COMMON CORE MATHEMATICS

NEW YORK EDITION

Grade 4, Module 1: Place Value, Rounding, and Algorithms for Addition and Subtraction

COMMON CORE

JOSSEY-BASS
A Wiley Imprint
www.josseybass.com

Cover design by Chris Clary

Published by Jossey-Bass
A Wiley Brand
One Montgomery Street, Suite 1200, San Francisco, CA 94104-4594—www.josseybass.com

ISBN 978-1-118-79296-4

Printed in the United States of America
FIRST EDITION
PB Printing   10 9 8 7 6 5 4 3 2 1

WELCOME

Dear Teacher,

Thank you for your interest in Common Core's curriculum in mathematics. Common Core is a non-profit organization based in Washington, DC dedicated to helping K-12 public schoolteachers use the power of high-quality content to improve instruction.[1] We are led by a board of master teachers, scholars, and current and former school, district, and state education leaders. Common Core has responded to the Common Core State Standards' (CCSS) call for "content-rich curriculum"[2] by creating new, CCSS-based curriculum materials in mathematics, English Language Arts, history, and (soon) the arts. All of our materials are written by teachers who are among the nation's foremost experts on the new standards.

In 2012 Common Core won three contracts from the New York State Education Department to create a PreKindergarten–12th grade mathematics curriculum for the teachers of that state, and to conduct associated professional development. The book you hold contains a portion of that work. In order to respond to demand in New York and elsewhere, modules of the curriculum will continue to be published, on a rolling basis, as they are completed. This curriculum is based on New York's version of the CCSS (the CCLS, or Common Core Learning Standards). Common Core will be releasing an enhanced version of the curriculum this summer on our website, commoncore.org. That version also will be published by Jossey-Bass, a Wiley imprint.

Common Core's curriculum materials are not merely aligned to the new standards, they take the CCSS as their very foundation. Our work in math takes its shape from the expectations embedded in the new standards—including the instructional shifts and mathematical progressions, and the new expectations for student fluency, deep conceptual understanding, and application to real-life context. Similarly, our ELA and history curricula are deeply informed by the CCSS's new emphasis on close reading, increased use of informational text, and evidence-based writing.

Our curriculum is distinguished not only by its adherence to the CCSS. The math curriculum is based on a theory of teaching math that is proven to work. That theory posits that mathematical knowledge is most coherently and

---

1. Despite the coincidence of name, Common Core and the Common Core State Standards are not affiliated. Common Core was established in 2007, prior to the start of the Common Core State Standards Initiative, which was led by the National Governors Association and the Council for Chief State School Officers.

2. *Common Core State Standards for English Language Arts & Literacy in History/Social Studies, Science, and Technical Subjects* (Washington, DC: Common Core State Standards Initiative), 6.

effectively conveyed when it is taught in a sequence that follows the "story" of mathematics itself. This is why we call the elementary portion of this curriculum "The Story of Units," to be followed by "The Story of Ratios" in middle school, and "The Story of Functions" in high school. Mathematical concepts flow logically, from one to the next, in this curriculum. The sequencing has been joined with methods of instruction that have been proven to work, in this nation and abroad. These methods drive student understanding beyond process, to deep mastery of mathematical concepts. The goal of the curriculum is to produce students who are not merely literate, but fluent, in mathematics.

It is important to note that, as extensive as these curriculum materials are, they are not meant to be prescriptive. Rather, they are intended to provide a basis for teachers to hone their own craft through study, collaboration, training, and the application of their own expertise as professionals. At Common Core we believe deeply in the ability of teachers and in their central and irreplaceable role in shaping the classroom experience. We strive only to support and facilitate their important work.

The teachers and scholars who wrote these materials are listed beginning on the next page. Their deep knowledge of mathematics, of the CCSS, and of what works in classrooms defined this work in every respect. I would like to thank Louisiana State University professor of mathematics Scott Baldridge for the intellectual leadership he provides to this project. Teacher, trainer, and writer Robin Ramos is the most inspired math educator I've ever encountered. It is Robin and Scott's aspirations for what mathematics education in America *should* look like that is spelled out in these pages.

Finally, this work owes a debt to project director Nell McAnelly that is so deep I'm confident it never can be repaid. Nell, who leads LSU's Gordon A. Cain Center for STEM Literacy, oversees all aspects of our work for NYSED. She has spent days, nights, weekends, and many cancelled vacations toiling in her efforts to make it possible for this talented group of teacher-writers to produce their best work against impossible deadlines. I'm confident that in the years to come Scott, Robin, and Nell will be among those who will deserve to be credited with putting math instruction in our nation back on track.

Thank you for taking an interest in our work. Please join us at www.commoncore.org.

Lynne Munson
President and Executive Director
Common Core
Washington, DC
June 20, 2013

Common Core's K-5 Math Staff

Scott Baldridge, Lead Mathematician and Writer
Robin Ramos, Lead Writer, PreKindergarten-5
Jill Diniz, Lead Writer, 6-12
Ben McCarty, Mathematician

Nell McAnelly, Project Director
Tiah Alphonso, Associate Director
Jennifer Loftin, Associate Director
Catriona Anderson, Curriculum Manager,
  PreKindergarten-5

Sherri Adler, PreKindergarten
Debbie Andorka-Aceves, PreKindergarten

Kate McGill Austin, Kindergarten
Nancy Diorio, Kindergarten
Lacy Endo-Peery, Kindergarten
Melanie Gutierrez, Kindergarten
Nuhad Jamal, Kindergarten
Cecilia Rudzitis, Kindergarten
Shelly Snow, Kindergarten

Beth Barnes, First Grade
Lily Cavanaugh, First Grade
Ana Estela, First Grade
Kelley Isinger, First Grade
Kelly Spinks, First Grade
Marianne Strayton, First Grade
Hae Jung Yang, First Grade

Wendy Keehfus-Jones, Second Grade
Susan Midlarsky, Second Grade
Jenny Petrosino, Second Grade
Colleen Sheeron, Second Grade
Nancy Sommer, Second Grade
Lisa Watts-Lawton, Second Grade
MaryJo Wieland, Second Grade
Jessa Woods, Second Grade

Eric Angel, Third Grade
Greg Gorman, Third Grade
Susan Lee, Third Grade
Cristina Metcalf, Third Grade
Ann Rose Santoro, Third Grade
Kevin Tougher, Third Grade
Victoria Peacock, Third Grade
Saffron VanGalder, Third Grade

Katrina Abdussalaam, Fourth Grade
Kelly Alsup, Fourth Grade
Patti Dieck, Fourth Grade
Mary Jones, Fourth Grade
Soojin Lu, Fourth Grade
Tricia Salerno, Fourth Grade
Gail Smith, Fourth Grade
Eric Welch, Fourth Grade
Sam Wertheim, Fourth Grade
Erin Wheeler, Fourth Grade

Leslie Arceneaux, Fifth Grade
Adam Baker, Fifth Grade
Janice Fan, Fifth Grade
Peggy Golden, Fifth Grade
Halle Kananak, Fifth Grade
Shauntina Kerrison, Fifth Grade
Pat Mohr, Fifth Grade
Chris Sarlo, Fifth Grade

Additional Writers

Bill Davidson, Fluency Specialist
Robin Hecht, UDL Specialist
Simon Pfeil, Mathematician

Document Management Team

Tam Le, Document Manager
Jennifer Merchan, Copy Editor

GRADE 4 • MODULE 1

Table of Contents

GRADE 4 • MODULE 1

Place Value, Rounding, and Algorithms for Addition and Subtraction

Grade 4 • Module 1

Place Value, Rounding, and Algorithms for Addition and Subtraction

OVERVIEW

In this 25-day module of Grade 4, students extend their work with whole numbers. They begin with large numbers using familiar units (hundreds and thousands) and develop their understanding of millions by building knowledge of the pattern of *times ten* in the base ten system on the place value chart (**4.NBT.1**). They recognize that each sequence of three digits is read as hundreds, tens, and ones followed by the naming of the corresponding base thousand unit (thousand, million, billion).[1]

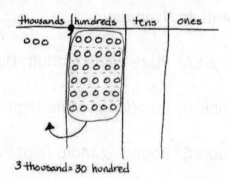

The place value chart will be fundamental in Topic A. Building upon their previous knowledge of *bundling,* students learn that 10 hundreds can be composed into 1 thousand and, therefore, 30 hundreds can be composed into 3 thousands because a digit's value is ten times what it would be one place to its right (**4.NBT.1**). Conversely, students learn to recognize that in a number such as 7,777 each 7 has a value that is 10 times the value of its neighbor to the immediate right. 1 thousand can be decomposed into 10 hundreds, therefore 7 thousands can be decomposed into 70 hundreds.

Similarly, multiplying by 10 will shift digits one place to the left, and dividing by 10 will shift digits one place to the right.

$$3,000 = 300 \times 10 \qquad 3,000 \div 10 = 300$$

In Topic B, students use place value as a basis for comparison of whole numbers. Although this is not a new topic, it becomes more complex because the numbers are larger. For example, it becomes clear that 34,156 is 3 thousand greater than 31,156.

$$34,156 > 31,156$$

Comparison leads directly into rounding, where their skill with isolating units is applied and extended. Rounding to the nearest ten and hundred was mastered with 3 digit numbers in Grade 3. Now Grade 4 students moving into Topic C learn to round to any place value (**4.NBT.3**) initially using the vertical number line though ultimately moving away from the visual model altogether. Topic C also includes word problems where students apply rounding to real life situations.

---

[1] Grade 4 expectations in the NBT standards domain, however, are limited to whole numbers less than or equal to 1,000,000.

In Grade 4, students become fluent with the standard algorithms for addition and subtraction. In Topics D and E students focus on single like-unit calculations (ones with ones, thousands with thousands, etc.) at times requiring the composition of greater units when adding (10 hundreds are composed into 1 thousand) and decomposition into smaller units when subtracting (1 thousand is decomposed into 10 hundreds) (**4.NBT.4**). Throughout these topics, students will apply their algorithmic knowledge to solve word problems. Also, students use a variable to represent the unknown quantity.

The module culminates with multi-step word problems in Topic F (**4.OA.3**). Tape diagrams are used throughout the topic to model additive compare problems like the one exemplified below. These diagrams facilitate deeper comprehension and serve as a way to support the reasonableness of an answer.

A goat produces 5,212 gallons of milk a year. The cow produces 17,279 gallons a year. How much more milk does the goat need to produce to make the same amount of milk as a cow?

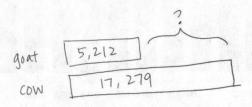

$$17,279 - 5,212 = \_\_\_\_$$

The goat needs to produce _____ more gallons of milk a year.

The mid-module assessment will follow Topic C. The end-of-module assessment follows Topic F.

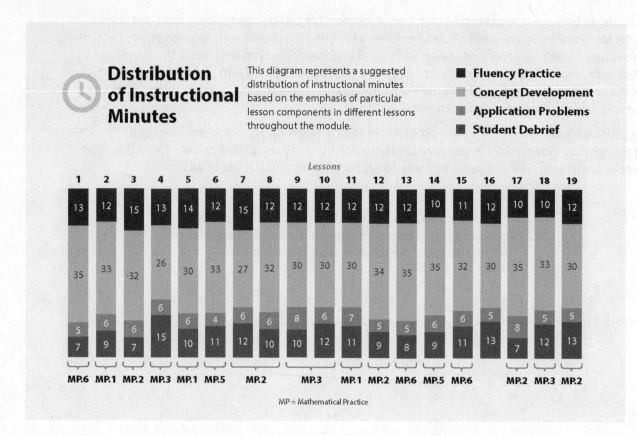

Focus Grade Level Standards

Use the four operations with whole numbers to solve problems.[2]

4.OA.3   Solve multistep word problems posed with whole numbers and having whole-number answers using the four operations, including problems in which remainders must be interpreted. Represent these problems using equations with a letter standing for the unknown quantity. Assess the reasonableness of answers using mental computation and estimation strategies including rounding.

Generalize place value understanding for multi-digit whole numbers. (Grade 4 expectations are limited to whole numbers less than or equal to 1,000,000.)

4.NBT.1   Recognize that in a multi-digit whole number, a digit in one place represents ten times what it represents in the place to its right. *For example, recognize that 700 ÷ 70 = 10 by applying concepts of place value and division.*

---

[2]Only addition and subtraction multi-step word problems are addressed in this module. The balance of this cluster is addressed in Modules 3 and 7.

4.NBT.2   Read and write multi-digit whole numbers using base-ten numerals, number names, and expanded form. Compare two multi-digit numbers based on meanings of the digits in each place, using >, =, and < symbols to record the results of comparisons.

4.NBT.3   Use place value understanding to round multi-digit whole numbers to any place.

Use place value understanding and properties of operations to perform multi-digit arithmetic.[3]

4.NBT.4   Fluently add and subtract multi-digit whole numbers using the standard algorithm.

Foundational Standards

3.OA.8   Solve two-step word problems using the four operations. Represent these problems using equations with a letter standing for the unknown quantity. Assess the reasonableness of answers using mental computation and estimation strategies including rounding. [4]

3.NBT.1   Use place value understanding to round whole numbers to the nearest 10 or 100.

3.NBT.2   Fluently add and subtract within 1000 using strategies and algorithms based on place value, properties of operations, and/or the relationship between addition and subtraction.

Focus Standards for Mathematical Practice

MP.1   **Make sense of problems and persevere in solving them.** Students use the place value chart to draw diagrams of the relationship between a digit's value and what it would be one place to its right, for instance, by representing 3 thousands as 30 hundreds. Students also use the place value chart to compare very large numbers.

MP.2   **Reason abstractly and quantitatively.** Students make sense of quantities and their relationships as they use both special strategies and the standard addition algorithm to add and subtract multi-digit numbers. Students also decontextualize when they represent problems symbolically and contextualize when they consider the value of the units used and understand the meaning of the quantities as they compute.

MP.3   **Construct viable arguments and critique the reasoning of others.** Students construct arguments as they use the place value chart and model single- and multi-step problems. Students also use the standard algorithm as a general strategy to add and subtract multi-digit numbers when a special strategy is not suitable.

MP.5   **Use appropriate tools strategically.** Students decide on the appropriatness of using special strategies or the standard algorithm when adding and subtracting multi-digit numbers.

MP.6   **Attend to precision.** Students use the place value chart to represent digits and their values as they compose and decompose base ten units.

---

[3] The balance of this cluster is addressed in Modules 3 and 7.

[4] This standard is limited to problems posed with whole numbers and having whole-number answers; students should know how to perform operations in the conventional order when there are no parentheses to specify a particular order, i.e., the Order of Operations.

COMMON CORE™

| Module 1: | Place Value, Rounding, and Algorithms for Addition and Subtraction |
| Date: | 6/27/13 |

v

Overview of Module Topics and Lesson Objectives

Standards		Topics and Objectives		Days
4.NBT.1 **4.NBT.2** 4.OA.1	A	**Place Value of Multi-Digit Whole Numbers**		4
		Lesson 1:	Interpret a multiplication equation as a comparison.	
		Lesson 2:	Recognize a digit represents 10 times the value of what it represents in the place to its right.	
		Lesson 3:	Name numbers within 1 million by building understanding of the place value chart and placement of commas for naming base thousand units.	
		Lesson 4:	Read and write multi-digit numbers using base ten numerals, number names, and expanded form.	
4.NBT.2	B	**Comparing Multi-Digit Whole Numbers**		2
		Lesson 5:	Compare numbers based on meanings of the digits, using >,<, or = to record the comparison.	
		Lesson 6:	Find 1, 10, and 100 thousand more and less than a given number.	
4.NBT.3	C	**Rounding Multi-Digit Whole Numbers**		4
		Lesson 7:	Round multi-digit numbers to the thousands place using the vertical number line.	
		Lesson 8:	Round multi-digit numbers to any place using the vertical number line.	
		Lesson 9:	Use place value understanding to round multi-digit numbers to any place value.	
		Lesson 10:	Use place value understanding to round multi-digit numbers to any place value using real world applications.	
		Mid-Module Assessment: Topics A–C (review content 1 day, assessment ½ day, return ½ day, remediation or further applications 1 day)		3
4.OA.3 **4.NBT.4** 4.NBT.1 4.NBT.2	D	**Multi-Digit Whole Number Addition**		2
		Lesson 11:	Use place value understanding to fluently add multi-digit whole numbers using the standard addition algorithm and apply the algorithm to solve word problems using tape diagrams.	
		Lesson 12:	Solve multi-step word problems using the standard addition algorithm modeled with tape diagrams and assess the reasonableness of answers using rounding.	

Standards		Topics and Objectives	Days
4.OA.3 **4.NBT.4** 4.NBT.1 4.NBT.2	E	**Multi-Digit Whole Number Subtraction** Lesson 13: Use place value understanding to decompose to smaller units once using the standard subtraction algorithm, and apply the algorithm to solve word problems using tape diagrams. Lesson 14: Use place value understanding to decompose to smaller units up to 3 times using the standard subtraction algorithm, and apply the algorithm to solve word problems using tape diagrams. Lesson 15: Use place value understanding to fluently decompose to smaller units multiple times in any place using the standard subtraction algorithm, and apply the algorithm to solve word problems using tape diagrams. Lesson 16: Solve two-step word problems using the standard subtraction algorithm fluently modeled with tape diagrams and assess the reasonableness of answers using rounding.	4
4.OA.3 4.NBT.1 4.NBT.2 4.NBT.4	F	**Addition and Subtraction Word Problems** Lesson 17: Solve additive compare word problems modeled with tape diagrams. Lesson 18: Solve multi-step word problems modeled with tape diagrams and assess the reasonableness of answers using rounding. Lesson 19: Create and solve multi-step word problems from given tape diagrams and equations.	3
		End-of-Module Assessment: Topics A through F (review content 1 day, assessment ½ day, return ½ day, remediation or further application 1 day)	3
Total Number of Instructional Days			25

Terminology

New or Recently Introduced Terms

- Ten thousands, hundred thousands (as places on the place value chart)
- One millions, ten millions, hundred millions (as places on the place value chart)
- Algorithm
- Variable

Module 1:   Place Value, Rounding, and Algorithms for Addition and Subtraction
Date: 6/27/13

Familiar Terms and Symbols[5]

- Sum (answer to an addition problem)
- Difference (answer to a subtraction problem)
- Rounding (approximating the value of a given number)
- Place value (the numerical value that a digit has by virtue of its position in a number)
- Digit (a numeral between 0 and 9)
- Standard form (a number written in the format: 135)
- Expanded form (e.g., 100 + 30 + 5 = 135)
- Word form (e.g., one hundred thirty-five)
- Tape diagram (bar diagram)
- Number line (a line marked with numbers at evenly spaced intervals)
- Bundling, making, renaming, changing, exchanging, regrouping, trading (e.g. exchanging 10 ones for 1 ten)
- Unbundling, breaking, renaming, changing, regrouping, trading (e.g. exchanging 1 ten for 10 ones)
- =, <, > (equal, less than, greater than)
- Number sentence (e.g., 4 + 3 = 7)

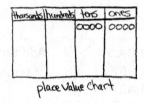

place value chart

Suggested Tools and Representations

- Place value charts (at least one per student for an insert in their personal board)
- Place value cards: one large set per classroom including 7 place values
- Number lines (a variety of templates) and a large one for the back wall of the classroom

number line

Suggested Methods of Instructional Delivery

Directions for Administration of Sprints

Sprints are designed to develop fluency. They should be fun, adrenaline-rich activities that intentionally build energy and excitement. A fast pace is essential. During Sprint administration, teachers assume the role of athletic coaches. A rousing routine fuels students' motivation to do their personal best. Student recognition of increasing success is critical, and so every improvement is celebrated.

One Sprint has two parts with closely related problems on each. Students complete the two parts of the Sprint in quick succession with the goal of improving on the second part, even if only by one more.

With practice, the following routine takes about 8 minutes.

---

[5] These are terms and symbols students have used or seen previously.

Sprint A

Pass *Sprint A* out quickly, face down on student desks with instructions to not look at the problems until the signal is given. (Some Sprints include words. If necessary, prior to starting the Sprint quickly review the words so that reading difficulty does not slow students down.)

T: You will have 60 seconds to do as many problems as you can.

T: I do not expect you to finish all of them. Just do as many as you can, your personal best. (If some students are likely to finish before time is up, assign a number to *count by* on the back.)

T: Take your mark! Get set! THINK! (When you say THINK, students turn their papers over and work furiously to finish as many problems as they can in 60 seconds. Time precisely.)

After 60 seconds:

T: Stop! Circle the last problem you did. I will read just the answers. If you got it right, call out "Yes!" and give a fist pump. If you made a mistake, circle it. Ready?

T: (Energetically, rapid-fire call the first answer.)

S: Yes!

T: (Energetically, rapid-fire call the second answer.)

S: Yes!

Repeat to the end of *Sprint A*, or until no one has any more correct. If need be, read the *count by* answers in the same way you read Sprint answers. Each number *counted by* on the back is considered a correct answer.

T: Fantastic! Now write the number you got correct at the top of your page. This is your personal goal for Sprint B.

T: How many of you got 1 right? (All hands should go up.)

T: Keep your hand up until I say the number that is 1 more than the number you got right. So, if you got 14 correct, when I say 15 your hand goes down. Ready?

T: (Quickly.) How many got 2 correct? 3? 4? 5? (Continue until all hands are down.)

Optional routine, depending on whether or not your class needs more practice with *Sprint A*:

T: I'll give you one minute to do more problems on this half of the Sprint. If you finish, stand behind your chair. (As students work you might have the person who scored highest on *Sprint A* pass out *Sprint B*.)

T: Stop! I will read just the answers. If you got it right, call out "Yes!" and give a fist pump. If you made a mistake, circle it. Ready? (Read the answers to the first half again as students stand.)

Movement

To keep the energy and fun going, always do a stretch or a movement game in between Sprint A and B. For example, the class might do jumping jacks while skip counting by 5 for about 1 minute. Feeling invigorated, students take their seats for *Sprint B*, ready to make every effort to complete more problems this time.

| Module 1: | Place Value, Rounding, and Algorithms for Addition and Subtraction |
| Date: | 6/27/13 |

Sprint B

Pass *Sprint B* out quickly, face down on student desks with instructions to not look at the problems until the signal is given. (Repeat the procedure for *Sprint A* up through the show of hands for how many right.)

T: Stand up if you got more correct on the second Sprint than on the first.

S: (Students stand.)

T: Keep standing until I say the number that tells how many more you got right on Sprint B. So if you got 3 more right on Sprint B than you did on Sprint A, when I say 3 you sit down. Ready? (Call out numbers starting with 1. Students sit as the number by which they improved is called. Celebrate the students who improved most with a cheer.)

T: Well done! Now take a moment to go back and correct your mistakes. Think about what patterns you noticed in today's Sprint.

T: How did the patterns help you get better at solving the problems?

T: Rally Robin your thinking with your partner for 1 minute. Go!

Rally Robin is a style of sharing in which partners trade information back and forth, one statement at a time per person, for about 1 minute. This is an especially valuable part of the routine for students who benefit from their friends' support to identify patterns and try new strategies.

Students may take Sprints home.

RDW or Read, Draw, Write (a Number Sentence and a Statement)

Mathematicians and teachers suggest a simple process applicable to all grades:

1) Read.
2) Draw and Label.
3) Write a number sentence (equation).
4) Write a word sentence (statement).

The more students participate in reasoning through problems with a systematic approach, the more they internalize those behaviors and thought processes.

- What do I see?
- Can I draw something?
- What conclusions can I make from my drawing?

Modeling with Interactive Questioning	Guided Practice	Independent Practice
The teacher models the whole process with interactive questioning, some choral response, and talk moves such as "What did Monique say, everyone?" After completing the problem, students might reflect with a partner on the steps they used to solve the problem. "Students, think back on what we did to solve this problem. What did we do first?" Students might then be given the same or similar problem to solve for homework.	Each student has a copy of the question. Though guided by the teacher, they work independently at times and then come together again. Timing is important. Students might hear, "You have 2 minutes to do your drawing." Or, "Put your pencils down. Time to work together again." The Debrief might include selecting different student work to share.	The students are given a problem to solve and possibly a designated amount of time to solve it. The teacher circulates, supports, and is thinking about which student work to show to support the mathematical objectives of the lesson. When sharing student work, students are encouraged to think about the work with questions such as, "What do you see Jeremy did?" "What is the same about Jeremy's work and Sara's work?" "How did Jeremy show the 3/7 of the students?" "How did Sara show the 3/7 of the students?"

Personal Boards

Materials Needed for Personal Boards

1 High Quality Clear Sheet Protector
1 piece of stiff red tag board 11" x 8 ¼"
1 piece of stiff white tag board 11" x 8 ¼"
1 3"x 3" piece of dark synthetic cloth for an eraser
1 Low Odor Blue Dry Erase Marker: Fine Point

Directions for Creating Personal Boards

Cut your white and red tag to specifications. Slide into the sheet protector. Store your eraser on the red side. Store markers in a separate container to avoid stretching the sheet protector.

Frequently Asked Questions About Personal Boards

Why is one side red and one white?

The white side of the board is the "paper." Students generally write on it and if working individually then turn the board over to signal to the teacher they have completed their work. The teacher then says, "Show me your boards," when most of the class is ready.

What are some of the benefits of a personal board?

- The teacher can respond quickly to a hole in student understandings and skills. "Let's do some of these on our personal boards until we have more mastery."

- Student can erase quickly so that they do not have to suffer the evidence of their mistake.

- They are motivating. Students love both the drill and thrill capability and the chance to do story problems with an engaging medium.

- Checking work gives the teacher instant feedback about student understanding.

What is the benefit of this personal board over a commercially purchased dry erase board?

- It is much less expensive.

- Templates such as place value charts, number bond mats, hundreds boards, and number lines can be stored between the two pieces of tag for easy access and reuse.

- Worksheets, story problems, and other problem sets can be done without marking the paper so that students can work on the problems independently at another time.

- Strips with story problems, number lines, and arrays can be inserted and still have a full piece of paper to write on.

- The red versus white side distinction clarifies your expectations. When working collaboratively, there is no need to use the red. When working independently, the students know how to keep their work private.

- The sheet protector can be removed so that student work can be projected on an overhead.

Scaffolds[6]

The scaffolds integrated into *A Story of Units* give alternatives for how students access information as well as express and demonstrate their learning. Strategically placed margin notes are provided within each lesson elaborating on the use of specific scaffolds at applicable times. They address many needs presented by English language learners, students with disabilities, students performing above grade level, and students performing below grade level. Many of the suggestions are organized by Universal Design for Learning (UDL) principles and are applicable to more than one population. To read more about the approach to differentiated instruction in *A Story of Units,* please refer to "How to Implement *A Story of Units.*"

---

[6] Students with disabilities may require Braille, large print, audio, or special digital files. Please visit the website, www.p12.nysed.gov/specialed/aim, for specific information on how to obtain student materials that satisfy the National Instructional Materials Accessibility Standard (NIMAS) format.

Assessment Summary

Type	Administered	Format	Standards Addressed
Mid-Module Assessment Task	After Topic C	Constructed response with rubric	4.NBT.1 4.NBT.2 4.NBT.3
End-of-Module Assessment Task	After Topic F	Constructed response with rubric	4.NBT.1 4.NBT.2 4.NBT.3 4.NBT.4 4.OA.3

Topic A

Place Value of Multi-Digit Whole Numbers

4.NBT.1, **4.NBT.2**, 4.OA.1

Focus Standard:	4.NBT.1	Recognize that in a multi-digit whole number, a digit in one place represents ten times what it represents in the place to its right. *For example, recognize that 700 ÷ 70 = 10 by applying concepts of place value and division.*
	4.NBT.2	Read and write multi-digit whole numbers using base-ten numerals, number names, and expanded form. Compare two multi-digit numbers based on meanings of the digits in each place, using >, =, and < symbols to record the results of comparisons.
Instructional Days:	4	
Coherence -Links from:	G3–M2	Place Value and Problem Solving with Units of Measure
-Links to:	G5–M1	Place Value and Decimal Fractions

In Topic A, students build the place value chart to 1 million and learn the relationship between each place value as *10 times* the value of the place to the right. Students manipulate numbers to see this relationship, such as 30 hundreds can be composed as 3 thousands. Conversely students decompose numbers to see that 7 thousands is the same as 70 hundreds. As students build the place value chart into thousands and up to 1 million, the sequence of 3 digits will be emphasized. They become familiar with the base thousand unit names up to 1 billion. Students fluently write numbers in multiple formats: as digits, in unit form, as words, and in expanded form up to 1 million.

A Teaching Sequence Towards Mastery of Place Value of Multi-Digit Whole Numbers

Objective 1: Interpret a multiplication equation as a comparison.
(Lesson 1)

Objective 2: Recognize a digit represents 10 times the value of what it represents in the place to its right.
(Lesson 2)

Objective 3: Name numbers within 1 million by building understanding of the place value chart and placement of commas for naming base thousand units.
(Lesson 3)

Objective 4: Read and write multi-digit numbers using base ten numerals, number names, and expanded form.
(Lesson 4)

Lesson 1

Objective: Interpret a multiplication equation as a comparison.

Suggested Lesson Structure

Fluency Practice	(13 minutes)
Application Problem	(5 minutes)
Concept Development	(35 minutes)
Student Debrief	(7 minutes)
Total Time	**(60 minutes)**

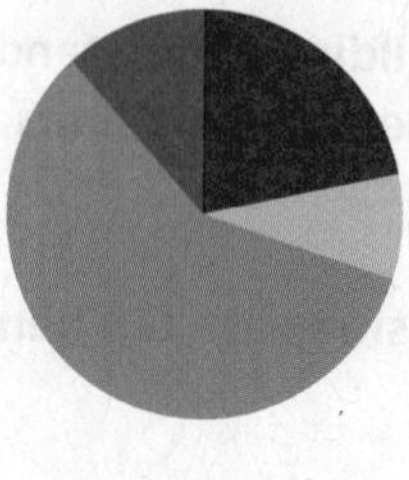

Fluency Practice (13 minutes)

- Multiply and Divide by 10 **4.NBT.1** (10 minutes)
- Place Value **4.NBT.2** (3 minutes)

Sprint: Multiply and Divide by 10 (10 minutes)

Materials: (S) Multiply and Divide by 10 Sprint

Note: Reviewing this fluency will acclimate students to the Sprint routine, a vital component of the fluency program.

Place Value (3 minutes)

Materials: (S) Personal white boards, place value chart

Note: Reviewing and practicing place value skills in isolation will prepare students for success in multiplying different place value units during the lesson.

T: (Project place value chart to the thousands.) Show 4 ones in number disks. Write the number below it.

S: (Students draw 4 ones disks and write 4 below it.)

T: Show 4 ten disks and write the number below it.

S: (Students draw 4 ten disks and write 4 at the bottom of the tens column.)

T: Say the number in unit form.

S: 4 tens 4 ones.

NOTES ON MULTIPLE MEANS FOR ACTION AND EXPRESSION:

For the place value fluency drill, students may represent ones, etc., using counters rather than drawing.

Others may benefit from the opportunity to practice simulataneously speaking and showing units (e.g., tens).

Provide sentence frames to support oral response, such as "_____tens_____ones is _____ (standard form) _____."

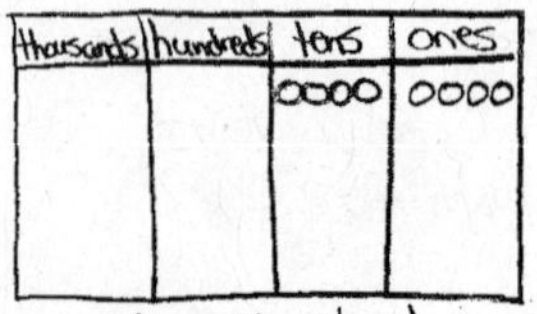

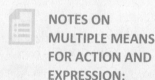

place value chart

T: Say the number in standard form.

S: 44.

Continue for the following possible sequence: 2 tens 3 ones, 2 hundreds 3 ones, 2 thousands 3 hundreds, 2 thousands 3 tens, and 2 thousands 3 hundreds 5 tens and 4 ones.

Application Problem (5 minutes)

Ben has a rectangular area 9 meters long and 6 meters wide. He wants a fence that will go around it as well as grass sod to cover it. How many meters of fence will he need? How many square meters of grass sod will he need to cover the entire area?

NOTES ON
MULTIPLE MEANS OF
ENGAGEMENT:

Enhance the relevancy of the Application Problem by substituting names, settings, and tasks to reflect your students and their experiences.

Set individual student goals and expectations. While some students may successfully solve for area and perimeter in 5 minutes, others may solve for one, while others may solve for both and compose their own Application Problem.

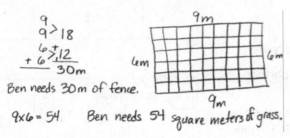

Note: As the first lesson of the year, this application problem reviews area and perimeter, multiplication, and addition—all important concepts from Grade 3. This problem can be extended after the Concept Development by asking students to find an area 10 times as much as the grass sod, or to find a perimeter 10 times as wide and 10 times as long.

Concept Development (35 minutes)

Materials: (T) Base ten disks: ones, tens, hundreds, and thousands (S) Personal white boards

Problem 1

1 ten is 10 times as many as 1 one.

T: (Have a place value chart ready. Draw or place 1 unit into the ones place.)

T: How many units do I have?

S: 1.

T: What is the name of this unit?

S: A one.

T: Count the ones with me. (Draw ones as they do so.)

S: 1 one, 2 ones, 3 ones, 4 ones, 5 ones...10 ones.

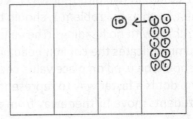

COMMON CORE™

Lesson 1:   Interpret a multiplication equation as a comparison.
Date: 6/28/13

1.A.4

© 2013 Common Core, Inc. All rights reserved. commoncore.org

MP.6

T: 10 ones. What larger unit can I make?

S: 1 ten.

T: I change 10 ones for 1 ten. We say, "1 ten is 10 times as much as 1 one." Tell your partner what we say and what that means. Use the model to help you.

S: 10 ones make 1 ten. → 10 times 1 one is 1 ten or 10 ones. → We say 1 ten is 10 times as many as 1 one.

Problem 2

One hundred is 10 times as much as 1 ten.

Quickly repeat the above process with 10 copies of 1 ten.

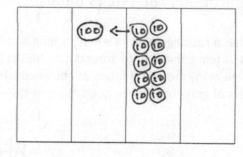

Problem 3

One thousand is 10 times as much as 1 hundred.

Quickly repeat the above process with 10 copies of 1 hundred.

T: Discuss the patterns you have noticed with your partner.

S: 10 ones makes 1 ten. 10 tens make 1 hundred. 10 hundreds make 1 thousand. → Every time we get 10 we bundle and make a bigger unit. → We copy a unit 10 times to make the next larger unit. → If we take any of the place value units, the next unit on the left is ten times as many.

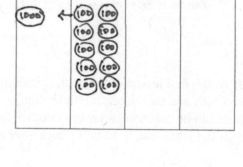

T: Let's review the multiplication pattern that matches our models and 10 times as many words.

Display the following information for student reference:

1 ten = 10 x 1 one	(Read, as "1 ten is 10 times as much as 1 one.")
1 hundred = 10 x 1 ten	(Say, "1 hundred is 10 times as much as 1 ten.")
1 thousand = 10 x 1 hundred	(Say, "1 thousand is 10 times as much as 1 hundred.")

Problem 4

Model on the place value chart and as equations 10 times as much as 2 ones.

Note: Number disks are used as models throughout the curriculum and can be represented in two different ways. A disk with a value labeled inside of it, such as in Problem 1, should be drawn or placed on a place value chart with no headings. The value of the disk in its appropriate column indicates the column heading. A number disk drawn as a dot should be used on place value charts with headings, as in Problem 4. The dot is a faster way to represent the number disk and is used as students move further away from a concrete stage of learning.

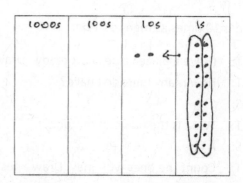

Lesson 1:   Interpret a multiplication equation as a comparison.
Date: 6/28/13

1.A.5

T: Draw place value disks as dots. Because you are using dots, label your columns with the unit value.

T: Represent 2 ones. Solve to find 10 times as many as 2 ones. Work together.

S: (Students work. Circulate as they do so.)

T: 10 times as many as 2 ones is?

S: 20 ones → 2 tens.

T: Explain this number sentence to your partner using your model.

10 × 2 ones = 20 ones = 2 tens

Repeat the process with 10 times as many as 4 tens.

10 × 4 tens = 40 tens = 4 hundreds

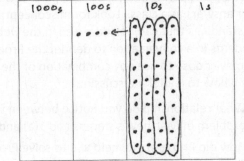

Problem 5

Model as an equation 10 times as many as 7 hundreds.

T: Write an equation and solve for 10 times as many as 7 hundreds.

Circulate and assist students as necessary.

T: Show me your boards. Read your equation.

S: 10 times 7 hundreds equals 70 hundreds equals 7 thousands.

10 × 7 hundreds = 70 hundreds = 7 thousands

Problem Set (10 minutes)

Students should do their personal best to complete the Problem Set within the allotted 10 minutes. Some problems do not specify a method for solving. This is an intentional reduction of scaffolding that invokes MP.5, Use Appropriate Tools Strategically. Students should solve these problems using the RDW approach used for Application Problems.

For some classes, it may be appropriate to modify the assignment by specifying which problems students should work on first. With this option, let the careful sequencing of the Problem Set guide your selections so that problems continue to be scaffolded. Balance word problems with other problem types to ensure a range of practice. Assign incomplete problems for homework or at another time during the day.

Challenge quick finishers to write their own 10 times as many statements similar to Problems 2 and 5.

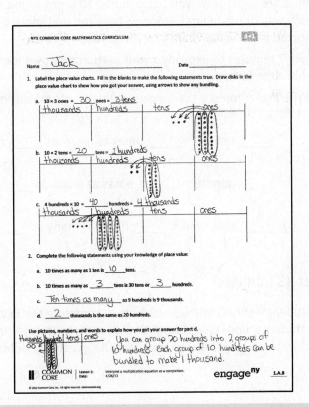

Lesson 1:   Interpret a multiplication equation as a comparison.
Date: 6/28/13

1.A.6

Student Debrief (7 minutes)

Lesson Objective: Interpret a multiplication equation as a comparison.

Invite students to review their solutions for the Problem Set and the totality of the lesson experience. They should check work by comparing answers with a partner before going over answers as a class. Look for misconceptions or misunderstandings that can be addressed in the Debrief. Guide students in a conversation to debrief the Problem Set. You may choose to use any combination of the questions below to lead the discussion.

- What relationship do you notice between the problem of Matthew's stamps and 1(a) and 1(b)?

- How did Problem 1(c) help you to solve Problem 4 about Jane's savings?

- In Problem 5 which solution proved most difficult to find? Why?

- How does the answer about Sarah's age and her grandfather's age relate to our lesson's objective?

- What are some ways you could model 10 times as many? What are the benefits and drawbacks of each way of modelling? (Money, base ten materials, disks, labeled drawings of disks, dots on a labeled place value chart, tape diagram.)

- Take 2 minutes to explain to your partner what we learned about the value of each unit as we move from right to left.

- Write and complete the following statements in your math journal:

    _____ ten is _____ times as many as _____ one

    _____ hundred is _____ times as many as _____ ten

    _____ thousand is _____ times as many as _____ hundred

Exit Ticket (3 minutes)

After the Student Debrief, instruct students to complete the Exit Ticket. A review of their work will help you assess the students' understanding of the concepts that were presented in the lesson today and plan more effectively for future lessons. You may read the questions aloud to the students.

Lesson 1:   Interpret a multiplication equation as a comparison.
Date: 6/28/13

1.A.7

A

Correct _____

Multiply or divide.

1	2 x 10 =		23	__ x 10 = 100	
2	3 x 10 =		24	__ x 10 = 20	
3	4 x 10 =		25	__ x 10 = 30	
4	5 x 10 =		26	100 ÷ 10 =	
5	1 x 10 =		27	50 ÷ 10 =	
6	20 ÷ 10 =		28	10 ÷ 10 =	
7	30 ÷ 10 =		29	20 ÷ 10 =	
8	50 ÷ 10 =		30	30 ÷ 10 =	
9	10 ÷ 10 =		31	__ x 10 = 60	
10	40 ÷ 10 =		32	__ x 10 = 70	
11	6 x 10 =		33	__ x 10 = 90	
12	7 x 10 =		34	__ x 10 = 80	
13	8 x 10 =		35	70 ÷ 10 =	
14	9 x 10 =		36	90 ÷ 10 =	
15	10 x 10 =		37	60 ÷ 10 =	
16	80 ÷ 10 =		38	80 ÷ 10 =	
17	70 ÷ 10 =		39	11 x 10 =	
18	90 ÷ 10 =		40	110 ÷ 10 =	
19	60 ÷ 10 =		41	30 ÷ 10 =	
20	100 ÷ 10 =		42	120 ÷ 10 =	
21	__ x 10 = 50		43	14 x 10 =	
22	__ x 10 = 10		44	140 ÷ 10 =	

© Bill Davidson

COMMON CORE™ Lesson 1: Interpret a multiplication equation as a comparison.
Date: 6/28/13

B

Improvement _____   # Correct _____

Multiply or divide.

1	1 x 10 =		23	___ x 10 = 20	
2	2 x 10 =		24	___ x 10 = 100	
3	3 x 10 =		25	___ x 10 = 30	
4	4 x 10 =		26	20 ÷ 10 =	
5	5 x 10 =		27	10 ÷ 10 =	
6	30 ÷ 10 =		28	100 ÷ 10 =	
7	20 ÷ 10 =		29	50 ÷ 10 =	
8	40 ÷ 10 =		30	30 ÷ 10 =	
9	10 ÷ 10 =		31	___ x 10 = 30	
10	50 ÷ 10 =		32	___ x 10 = 40	
11	10 x 10 =		33	___ x 10 = 90	
12	6 x 10 =		34	___ x 10 = 70	
13	7 x 10 =		35	80 ÷ 10 =	
14	8 x 10 =		36	90 ÷ 10 =	
15	9 x 10 =		37	60 ÷ 10 =	
16	70 ÷ 10 =		38	70 ÷ 10 =	
17	60 ÷ 10 =		39	11 x 10 =	
18	80 ÷ 10 =		40	110 ÷ 10 =	
19	100 ÷ 10 =		41	120 x 10 =	
20	90 ÷ 10 =		42	120 ÷ 10 =	
21	___ x 10 = 10		43	13 x 10 =	
22	___ x 10 = 50		44	130 ÷ 10 =	

© Bill Davidson

Lesson 1:   Interpret a multiplication equation as a comparison.
Date: 6/28/13

1.A.9

Name _____   Date _____

1. Label the place value charts. Fill in the blanks to make the following statements true. Draw disks in the place value chart to show how you got your answer, using arrows to show any bundling.

a. 10 × 3 ones = _____ ones = _____

b. 10 × 2 tens = _____ tens = _____

c. 4 hundreds × 10 = _____ hundreds = _____

2. Complete the following statements using your knowledge of place value:

a. 10 times as many as 1 ten is _____ tens.

b. 10 times as many as _____ tens is 30 tens or _____ hundreds.

c. _____ as 9 hundreds is 9 thousands.

d. _____ thousands is the same as 20 hundreds.

Use pictures, numbers, and words to explain how you got your answer for Part (d).

3. Matthew has 30 stamps in his collection. Matthew's father has 10 times as many stamps as Matthew. How many stamps does Matthew's father have? Use numbers and words to explain how you got your answer.

4. Jane saved $800. Her sister has 10 times as much money. How much money does Jane's sister have? Use numbers and words to explain how you got your answer.

5. Fill in the blanks to make the statements true.

   a. 2 times as much as 4 is _____.

   b. 10 times as much as 4 is _____.

   c. 500 is 10 times as much as _____.

   d. 6,000 is _____ as 600.

6. Sarah is 9 years old. Sarah's grandfather is 90 years old. Sarah's grandfather is how many times as old as Sarah?

   Sarah's grandfather is _____ times as old as Sarah.

Name _____   Date _____

1. Use the number disks in the place value chart below to complete the following problems.

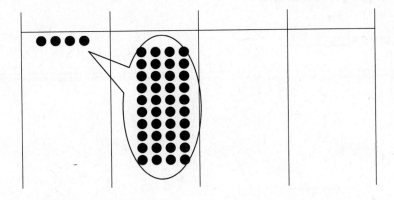

a. Label the place value chart.

b. Tell about the movement of the disks in the place value chart by filling in the blanks to make the following equation true and match what is happening in the place value chart.

_____ × 10 = _____ = _____

c. Write a statement about this place value chart using the words "10 times as many."

Name _____ Date _____

1. Label the place value charts. Fill in the blanks to make the following statements true. Draw disks in the place value chart to show how you got your answer.

   a. 10 × 4 ones = _____ ones = _____

   b. 10 × 2 tens = _____ tens = _____

   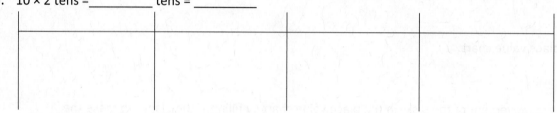

   c. 5 hundreds × 10 = _____ hundreds = _____

   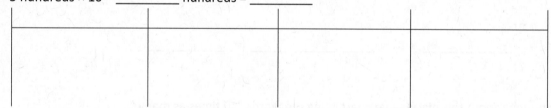

2. Complete the following statements using your knowledge of place value:

   a. 10 times as many as 1 hundred is _____ hundreds or _____ thousand.

   b. 10 times as many as _____ hundreds is 60 hundreds or _____ thousands.

   c. _____ as 8 hundreds is 8 thousands.

   d. _____ hundreds is the same as 4 thousands.

Use pictures, numbers, and words to explain how you got your answer for Part (d).

COMMON CORE™

Lesson 1: Interpret a multiplication equation as a comparison.
Date: 6/28/13

1.A.13

3. Katrina has 60 GB of storage on her tablet. Katrina's father has 10 times as much storage on his computer. How much storage does Katrina's father have? Use numbers and words to explain how you got your answer.

4. Katrina saved $200 to purchase her tablet. Her father spent 10 times as much money to buy his new computer. How much did her father's computer cost? Use numbers and words to explain how you got your answer.

5. Fill in the blanks to make the statements true.

   a. 4 times as much as 3 is _____.

   b. 10 times as much as 9 is _____.

   c. 700 is 10 times as much as _____.

   d. 8,000 is _____ as 800.

6. Tomas's grandfather is 100 years old. Tomas's grandfather is 10 times as old. How old is Tomas?

Lesson 2

Objective: Recognize a digit represents 10 times the value of what it represents in the place to its right.

Suggested Lesson Structure

■ Fluency Practice   (12 minutes)
▨ Application Problem   (6 minutes)
■ Concept Development   (33 minutes)
■ Student Debrief   (9 minutes)
   Total Time   **(60 minutes)**

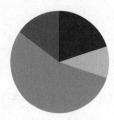

Fluency Practice (12 minutes)

- Skip-Counting **3.OA.7**   (4 minutes)
- Place Value **4.NBT.2**   (4 minutes)
- Multiply by 10 **4.NB5.1**   (4 minutes)

Skip Counting (4 minutes)

Note: Practicing skip-counting on the number line builds a foundation for accessing higher order concepts throughout the year.

Direct students to count by threes forward and backward to 36, focusing on the crossing-ten transitions.

Example: (3, 6, 9, 12, 9, 12, 9, 12, 15, 18, 21, 18, 21, 24, 27, 30, 27, 30, 33, 30, 33, 30, 33, 36...) The purpose of focusing on crossing the ten transitions is to help students to make the connection that, for example, when adding 3 to 9 that 9 + 1 is 10 and then 2 more is 12.

We see a similar purpose in counting down by threes; 12 − 2 is 10 and subtracting 1 more is 9. This work builds on the fluency work of previous grade levels. Students should understand that when crossing the tens that they, in essence, are regrouping.

Direct students to count by fours forward and backward to 48, focusing on the crossing ten transitions.

Place Value (4 minutes)

Materials: (S) Personal white boards with a place value chart to thousands

Note: Reviewing and practicing place value skills in isolation will prepare students for success in multiplying different place value units during the lesson.

Lesson 2:   Recognize a digit represents 10 times the value of what it represents
             in the place to its right.
Date: 6/28/13

1.A.15

T: (Project place value chart to the thousands place.) Show 5 tens in number disks and write the number below it.

Students draw 5 ten disks, write 5 below it and 0 in the ones column. (Draw to correct student misunderstanding.)

    T: Say the number in unit form.

    S: 5 tens.

    T: Say the number in standard form.

    S: 50.

Continue for the following possible sequence: 3 tens 2 ones, 4 hundreds 3 ones, 1 thousand 2 hundreds, 4 thousands 2 tens, 4 thousands 2 hundreds 3 tens and 5 ones.

Multiply by 10 (4 minutes)

Materials: (S) Personal white boards

Note: This fluency will review concepts learned in Lesson 1.

    T: (Project 10 ones x 10 = 1 _____.) Fill in the blank.

Students write 10 ones x 10 = 1 hundred.

    T: Say the multiplication sentence in standard form.

    S: 10 x 10 = 100.

Repeat for the following possible sequence 10 x _____ = 2 hundreds; 10 x _____ = 3 hundreds; 10 x _____ = 7 hundreds;

10 x 1 hundred = 1 _____; 10 x _____ = 2 thousands; 10 x _____ = 8 thousands;

10 x 10 thousands = _____.

Application Problem (6 minutes)

Amy is baking muffins. Each baking tray can hold 6 muffins.

    a. If Amy bakes 4 trays of muffins, how many muffins will she have all together?

    b. The corner bakery has made 10 times as many muffins as Amy baked. How many muffins did the bakery produce?

Bonus: If the corner bakery packages the muffins in boxes of 100, how many boxes of 100 could they make?

a) 6 x 4 = 24 muffins

b) 24 x 10 = 240 muffins

Bonus: 240 could make two groups of 100.

Note: This application problem builds on the concept from the previous lesson of *10 times as many*.

COMMON CORE™ | Lesson 2: Date: | Recognize a digit represents 10 times the value of what it represents in the place to its right. 6/28/13   1.A.16

© 2013 Common Core, Inc. All rights reserved. **commoncore.org**

Concept Development (33 minutes)

Materials: (S) Personal white boards

Problem 1

Multiply single units by 10 to build the place value chart to 1 million. Divide to reverse the process.

> T: On your board, write the multiplication sentence that shows the relationship between 1 hundred and 1 thousand.
>
> S: (Students write: 10 × 1 hundred = 10 hundreds = 1 thousand.)
>
> T: Draw number disks on your place value chart to find the value of 10 times 1 thousand.
>
> T: (Circulate.) I saw that Tessa drew 10 disks in the thousands column. What does that represent?
>
> S: 10 times 1 thousand equals 10 thousand.
> (10 × 1 thousand = 10 thousand.)

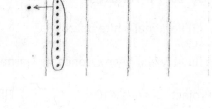

> T: How else can 10 thousand be represented?
>
> S: 10 thousand can be bundled because when you have 10 of one unit, you can bundle it and move it to the next column.
>
> T: (Point to the place value chart.) Can anyone think what the name of our next column after the thousands might be? (Students might share. Label the **ten thousands** column.)
>
> T: Now write a complete multiplication sentence to show 10 times the value of 1 thousand. Show how you regroup.

10 × 1 thousand = 10 thousand = 1 ten thousand

> T: On your place value chart, show what 10 times the value of 1 ten thousand equals.

Circulate and assist students as necessary.

> T: What is 10 times 1 ten thousand?
>
> S: 10 ten thousands. → 1 **hundred thousand**.
>
> T: That is our next larger unit.

10 × 1 ten thousand = 10 ten thousands = 1 hundred thousand

> T: To move another column to the left, what would be my next 10 times statement?
>
> S: 10 times 1 hundred thousand.
>
> T: Solve to find 10 times 1 hundred thousand.

Circulate and assist students as necessary.

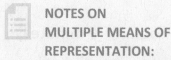

NOTES ON MULTIPLE MEANS OF REPRESENTATION:

Scaffold student understanding of the place value pattern by recording the following sentence frames:

- 10 x 1 one is 1 ten
- 10 x 1 ten is 1 hundred
- 10 x 1 hundred is 1 thousand
- 10 x 1 thousand is 1 ten thousand
- 10 x 1 ten thousand is 1 hundred thousand

Students may benefit from speaking this pattern chorally. Deepen understanding with prepared visuals (perhaps using a SMART board).

Lesson 2: Recognize a digit represents 10 times the value of what it represents in the place to its right.

Date: 6/28/13

1.A.17

T: 10 hundred thousands can be bundled and represented as **1 million**. Title your column and write the multiplication sentence.

10 × 1 hundred thousand = 10 hundred thousands = 1 million

After having built the place value chart by multiplying by ten, quickly review the process simply moving from right to left on the place value chart, and then reversing and moving left to right. (e.g., 2 tens times 10 equals 2 hundreds times 10 equals 2 thousands divided by 10 equals 2 hundreds divided by 10 equals 2 tens.)

Problem 2

Multiply multiple copies of one unit by 10 (e.g., 10 × 4 ten thousands).

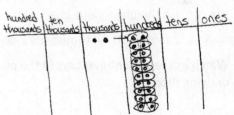

T: Draw number disks and write a multiplication sentence to show the value of 10 times 4 ten thousands.

T: 10 times 4 ten thousands is?

S: 40 ten thousands. → 4 hundred thousands.

T: Explain to your partner how you know this equation is true.

10 × 4 ten thousands = 40 ten thousands = 4 hundred thousands

Repeat with 10 × 3 hundred thousands.

Problem 3

Divide multiple copies of one unit by 10: 2 thousands ÷ 10. Solve in unit form: 2 thousands ÷ 10

T: What is the process for solving this division equation?

S: Use a place value chart. → Represent 2 thousands on a place value chart and then change for smaller units so we can divide.

T: What would our place value chart look like if we changed each thousand for 10 smaller units?

S: 20 hundreds. → 2 thousands can be changed to be 20 hundreds because 2 thousands and 20 hundreds are equal.

T: Solve for the answer.

S: 2 hundreds. → 2 thousands ÷ 10 is 2 hundreds because 2 thousands unbundled becomes 20 hundreds. → 20 hundreds divided by 10 is 2 hundreds.

2 thousands ÷ 10 = 20 hundreds ÷ 10 = 2 hundreds

Repeat with 3 hundred thousands ÷ 10.

Lesson 2:   Recognize a digit represents 10 times the value of what it represents
             in the place to its right.
Date: 6/28/13

1.A.18

Problem 4

Multiply and divide multiple copies of two different units by 10.

T: Draw number disks to show 3 hundreds and 2 tens.

T: Work in pairs to solve (write) 10 × (3 hundreds 2 tens).

T: I wrote (3 hundreds 2 tens) in parentheses to show it is one number.

Circulate as students work. Clarify that both hundreds and tens must be multiplied by 10.

T: What is your product?

S: 3 thousands 2 hundreds.

10 × (3 hundreds 2 tens) = 3 thousands 2 hundreds = 3,200

T: How could we write this in standard form?

S: 3,200

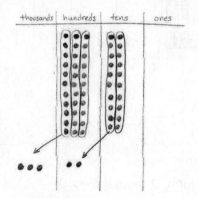

(4 ten thousands 2 tens) ÷ 10

T: In this equation we have two units. Explain how you will find your answer.

S: We can use the place value chart again and represent the unbundled units, then divide.

(4 ten thousands 2 tens) ÷ 10 = 4 thousands 2 ones = 4,002

T: Watch as I represent numbers in the place value chart to multiply or divide by ten, instead of drawing disks.

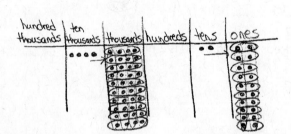

Repeat with 10 × (4 thousands 5 hundreds) and (7 hundreds 9 tens) ÷ 10.

Problem Set (10 minutes)

Students should do their personal best to complete the Problem Set within the allotted 10 minutes. For some classes, it may be appropriate to modify the assignment by specifying which problems they work on first. Some problems do not specify a method for solving. Students solve these problems using the RDW approach used for Application Problems.

Student Debrief (9 minutes)

Lesson Objective: Recognize a digit represents 10 times the value of what it represents in the place to its right.

Invite students to review their solutions for the Problem Set and the totality of the lesson experience. They should check work by comparing answers with a partner before going over answers as a class. Look for misconceptions or misunderstandings that can be addressed in the Debrief. Guide students in a conversation to debrief the Problem Set. You may choose to use any combination of the questions below to lead the discussion.

- How did we use patterns to predict the increasing units on the place value chart up to **1 million**? Can you predict the unit that is 10 times 1 million? 100 times 1 million?

- What happens when you multiply a number by 10? 1 **ten thousand** is what times 10? 1 **hundred thousand** is what times 10?

- Gail said that she noticed that when you multiply a number by 10, you shift the digits one place to the left and put a zero in the ones place. Is she correct?

- How can you use multiplication and division to describe the relationship between units on the place value chart? Use Problems 1(a) and 1(c) to help explain.

- Practice reading your answers in Problem 2 out loud. What similarities did you find in saying the numbers in unit form and standard form? Differences?

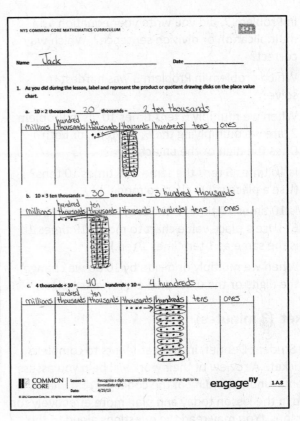

COMMON CORE™ | Lesson 2: | Recognize a digit represents 10 times the value of what it represents in the place to its right.
Date: | 6/28/13

© 2013 Common Core, Inc. All rights reserved. **commoncore.org**

1.A.20

- In Problem 7, did you write your equation as a multiplication or division sentence? Which way is correct?

- Which problem in Problem 3 was hardest to solve?

- When we multiply 6 tens times 10, as in Problem 2, are we multiplying the 6, the tens, or both? Does the digit or the unit change?

- Is 10 times 6 tens the same as 6 times 10 tens? (Use a place value chart to model.)

- Is 10 times 10 times 6 the same as 10 tens times 6? (Use a place value chart to model 10 times 10 is the same as 1 ten times 1 ten.)

- When we multiply or divide by 10 do we change the digits or the unit? Make a few examples.

Exit Ticket (3 minutes)

After the Student Debrief, instruct students to complete the Exit Ticket. A review of their work will help you assess the students' understanding of the concepts that were presented in the lesson today and plan more effectively for future lessons. You may read the questions aloud to the students.

COMMON CORE™

Lesson 2:

Date:

Recognize a digit represents 10 times the value of what it represents in the place to its right.

6/28/13

1.A.21

© 2013 Common Core, Inc. All rights reserved. commoncore.org

Name _____   Date _____

1. As you did during the lesson, label and represent the product or quotient drawing disks on the place value chart.

    a.   10 × 2 thousands = _____ thousands = _____

    b.   10 × 3 ten thousands = _____ ten thousands = _____

    c.   4 thousands ÷ 10 = _____ hundreds ÷ 10 = _____

COMMON CORE™   **Lesson 2:**   Recognize a digit represents 10 times the value of what it represents in the place to its right.

Date: 6/28/13   1.A.22

2. Fill in the blanks to complete each number sentence. Respond first in unit form, then in standard form.

Expression	Unit form	Standard Form
10 × 6 tens		
7 hundreds × 10		
3 thousands ÷ 10		
6 ten thousands ÷ 10		
10 x 4 thousands		

3. Fill in the blanks to complete each number sentence. Respond first in unit form, then in standard form.

Expression	Unit form	Standard Form
(4 tens 3 ones) x 10		
(2 hundreds 3 tens) × 10		
(7 thousands 8 hundreds) × 10		
(6 thousands 4 tens) ÷ 10		
(4 ten thousands 3 tens) ÷ 10		

4. Explain how you solved the last problem of Set 2. Use a place value chart to support your explanation.

COMMON CORE™

Lesson 2:   Recognize a digit represents 10 times the value of what it represents in the place to its right.

Date: 6/28/13

1.A.23

5. Explain how you solved the last problem of Set 3. Use a place value chart to support your explanation.

6. Jacob saved 2 thousand dollar bills, 4 hundred dollar bills, and 6 ten dollar bills to buy a car. The car costs 10 times as much as he has saved. How much does the car cost?

7. Last year the apple orchard experienced a drought and didn't produce many apples. But this year, the apple orchard produced 45 thousand granny smith apples and 9 hundred red delicious apples, which is 10 times as many apples as last year. How many apples did the orchard produce last year?

8. Planet Ruba has a population of 1 million aliens. Planet Zamba has 1 hundred thousand aliens.
    a. How many more aliens does Planet Ruba have than Planet Zamba?

    b. Write a sentence to compare the populations for each planet using the words "10 times as many."

	Lesson 2:	Recognize a digit represents 10 times the value of what it represents in the place to its right.	1.A.24
	Date:	6/28/13	

Name _____   Date _____

1. Fill in the blank to complete the number sentence. Respond with a numeral.

    a.   (4 ten thousands 6 hundreds) × 10 = _____

    b.   (8 thousands 2 tens) ÷ 10 = _____

2. The Carson family saved up $39,580 for a new home. The cost of their dream home is 10 times as much as they have saved. How much does their dream home cost?

COMMON CORE™

Lesson 2:   Recognize a digit represents 10 times the value of what it represents
             in the place to its right.
Date: 6/28/13

1.A.25

Name _____   Date _____

1. As you did during the lesson, label and represent the product or quotient drawing disks on the place value chart.

   a. 10 × 4 thousands = _____ thousands = _____

   b. 4 thousands ÷ 10 = _____ hundreds ÷ 10 = _____

2. Fill in the blanks to complete each number sentence. Respond first in unit form, then in standard form.

Expression	Unit Form	Standard Form
10 × 3 tens		
5 hundreds × 10		
9 ten thousands ÷ 10		
10 x 7 thousands		

COMMON CORE™   Lesson 2:   Recognize a digit represents 10 times the value of what it represents in the place to its right.   **1.A.26**

Date: 6/28/13

3. Fill in the blanks to complete each number sentence. Respond first in unit form, then in standard form.

Expression	Unit Form	Standard Form
(2 tens 1 one) x 10		
(5 hundreds 5 tens) × 10		
(2 thousands 7 tens) ÷ 10		
(4 ten thousands 8 hundreds) ÷ 10		

4. Emily collected $950 selling Girl Scout cookies all day Saturday. Emily's troop collected 10 times as much as she did. How much money did Emily's troop raise?

5. On Saturday, Emily made 10 times as much as on Monday. How much money did Emily collect on Monday?

COMMON CORE™

Lesson 2: Recognize a digit represents 10 times the value of what it represents in the place to its right.

Date: 6/28/13

1.A.27

Lesson 3

Objective: Name numbers within 1 million by building understanding of the place value chart and placement of commas for naming base thousand units.

Suggested Lesson Structure

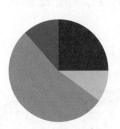

■ Fluency Practice   (15 minutes)
  Application Problem   (6 minutes)
■ Concept Development   (32 minutes)
■ Student Debrief   (7 minutes)
  Total Time   **(60 minutes)**

Fluency Practice (15 minutes)

- Multiply by 3 **3.OA.7**   (10 minutes)
- Place Value and Value **4.NBT.2**   (3 minutes)
- Base Ten Units **4.NBT.1**   (2 minutes)

Sprint: Multiply by 3 (10 minutes)

Materials: (S) Multiply by 3 Sprint

Note: This fluency will review a foundational third grade standard that will help students learn standard **4.NBT.5**.

Place Value and Value (3 minutes)

Note: Reviewing and practicing place value skills in isolation will prepare students for success in multiplying different place value units during the lesson.

- T: (Project the number 1,468,357 on a place value chart. Underline the 5.) Say the digit.
- S: 5.
- T: Say the place value of the 5.
- S: Tens.
- T: Say the value of 5 tens.
- S: 50.

**A NOTE
ON STANDARDS
ALIGNMENT:**

In this lesson, students extend past 1 million (**4.NBT** standards limit whole numbers less than or equal to 1 million) to establish a pattern of ones, tens, and hundreds within each base ten unit (thousands, millions, billions, trillions).

Calculations in following lessons are limited to less than or greater than 1 million.

If your students are not ready for this step, you might omit establishing the pattern, yet eternalize the units of base thousand.

| Lesson 3: | Name numbers within 1 million by building understanding of the place value chart and placement of commas for naming base thousand units. |
| Date: | 6/28/13 |

1.A.28

Repeat process, underlining 8, 4, 1, and 6.

Base Ten Units (2 minutes)

Note: This fluency will bolster students' place value proficiency while reviewing multiplication concepts learned in Lessons 1 and 2.

> T: (Project 2 tens =____.) Say the number in standard form.
>
> S: 2 tens = 20.

Repeat for possible sequence: 3 tens, 9 tens, 10 tens, 11, tens, 12 tens, 19 tens, 20 tens, 30, tens, 40 tens, 80 tens, 84 tens, and 65 tens.

Application Problem (6 minutes)

The school library has 10,600 books.
The town library has 10 times as many books.
How many books does the town library have?

Note: This application problem builds on the concept from the previous lesson of determining 10 times as much as a number.

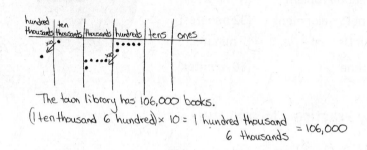

The town library has 106,000 books.
(1 ten thousand 6 hundred) × 10 = 1 hundred thousand 6 thousands = 106,000

Concept Development (32 minutes)

Materials: (S) Personal white boards with million-place value chart outline template

Note: Students will go beyond the **4.NBT** standard of using numbers less than or equal to 1 million to establish a pattern within the base ten units.

> T: In the last lesson we extended the place value chart to 1 million. Take a minute to label the place value headings on your place value chart.

Circulate and check all headings.

> T: Excellent. Now talk with your partner about similarities and differences you see in those heading names.
>
> S: I notice some words repeat, like ten, hundred, thousands. But, *ones* appears once. → I notice the thousand unit repeats 3 times—thousands, ten thousands, hundred thousands.

NOTES ON MULTIPLE MEANS FOR ACTION AND EXPRESSION:

Scaffold partner talk with sentence frames, such as,

"I notice _____."

"The place value headings are alike because _____."

"The place value headings are not alike because _____."

"The pattern I notice is _____."

"I notice the units _____."

Lesson 3:   Name numbers within 1 million by building understanding of the place value chart and placement of commas for naming base thousand units.

Date: 6/28/13

1.A.29

T: That's right! Beginning with thousands, we start naming new place value units by how many one thousands, ten thousands, and hundred thousands we have. What do you think the next unit might be called after 1 million?

S: **Ten millions.**

T: (Extend chart to the ten millions.) And the next?

S: **Hundred millions.**

T: (Extend chart again.) That's right! Just like with thousands, we name new units here in terms of how many one millions, ten millions, and hundred millions we have. 10 hundred millions gets renamed as 1 billion. Talk with your partner about what the next two place value units should be.

S: Ten billions, and hundred billions. → It works just like it does for thousands and millions!

Problem 1

Placing commas in and naming 3,608,430,325.

T: You've noticed a pattern: ones, tens and hundreds; one thousands, ten thousands, and hundred thousands; one millions, ten millions, and hundred millions; and so on. We use commas to indicate this grouping of units, taken 3 at a time. For example ten billion would be written: 10,000,000,000.

Write 3608430325.

T: Record this number in your place value chart and place the commas to show our groupings of units.

T: (Show 430,325 on a place value chart.) How many thousands are in this number?

S: 430.

T: 430 what?

S: 430 thousands.

T: Correct, we read this number as "four hundred thirty thousand, three hundred twenty-five."

T: (Extend chart and show 608,430,325.) How many millions are there in this number?

S: 608 millions.

T: Using what you know about our pattern in naming units, talk with your partner about how to name this number.

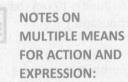

NOTES ON MULTIPLE MEANS FOR ACTION AND EXPRESSION:

Scaffold reading numbers into the hundred thousands with questioning, such as:

What's the value of the 3? 30 thousand. How many thousands altogether? 36 thousands. What's the value of the 8? 80. Add the remaining ones? 89. Read the whole number. Thirty-six thousand, eighty-nine.

Continue with similar numbers until students reach fluency. Alternate student recording numbers, modeling, and reading.

Lesson 3: Name numbers within 1 million by building understanding of the place value chart and placement of commas for naming base thousand units.

Date: 6/28/13

1.A.30

Problem 2

Add to make 10 of a unit and bundling up to 1 million.

T: What would happen if we combined 2 groups of 5 hundreds? With your partner draw number disks to solve. Use the largest unit possible to express your answer.

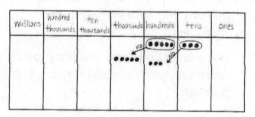

S: 2 groups of 5 hundreds equals 10 hundreds. →
It would make 10 hundreds, which can be bundled to make 1 thousand.

MP.2

T: Now, solve for 5 thousands plus 5 thousands. Bundle in order to express your answer using the largest unit possible.

S: 5 thousands plus 5 thousands equals 10 thousands. Bundle 10 thousands to make 1 ten thousand.

T: Solve for 4 ten thousands plus 6 ten thousands. Express your answer using the largest unit possible.

S: 4 ten thousands plus 6 ten thousands equals 10 ten thousands. Bundle 10 ten thousands to make 1 hundred thousand.

Continue renaming problems, showing regrouping as necessary.

3 hundred thousands + 7 hundred thousands

23 thousands + 4 ten thousands

43 ten thousands + 11 thousands

Problem 3

10 times as many with multiple units.

T: On your place value chart, model 5 hundreds and 3 tens with number disks. What is ten times 5 hundreds 3 tens?

S: (Students show.) 5 thousands 3 hundreds.

T: Model 5 thousands 3 hundreds with numbers on the place value chart.

S: 5,300.

T: Check your partner's work and remind him of the comma's role in this number.

T: With your partner solve this problem and write your answer in standard form.

Display 10 X 1 ten thousand 5 thousands 3 hundreds 2 ones = _____

S: 10 x 15,309 equals 153,090

Lesson 3:   Name numbers within 1 million by building understanding of the place value chart and placement of commas for naming base thousand units.

Date: 6/28/13

1.A.31

Problem Set (10 minutes)

Students should do their personal best to complete the Problem Set within the allotted 10 minutes. For some classes, it may be appropriate to modify the assignment by specifying which problems they work on first. Some problems do not specify a method for solving. Students solve these problems using the RDW approach used for Application Problems.

Student Debrief (7 minutes)

Lesson Objective: Name numbers within 1 million by building understanding of the place value chart and placement of commas for naming base thousand units.

Invite students to review their solutions for the Problem Set and the totality of the lesson experience.
They should check work by comparing answers with a partner before going over answers as a class. Look for misconceptions or misunderstandings that can be addressed in the Debrief. Guide students in a conversation to debrief the Problem Set. You may choose to use any combination of the questions below to lead the discussion.

- In Problem 1, how did you know where to place commas within a number?

- Read aloud the numbers in Problems 1(d) and 1(e) with your partner. What role do the commas have as you read across the number?

- How do place value understanding and the role of commas help you to read the value in the millions period that is represented by the number of millions, **ten millions**, and **hundred millions**?

- What did you discover as you solved Problem 3? How did part (a) help you to solve part (b)?

- How did you use the place value chart to help you compare unlike units in Problem 5?

- When might it be useful to omit commas? (Please refer to the UDL box for commas to guide your discussion.)

NOTES ON COMMAS:

Commas are optional for 4-digit numbers, as this supports visualization of the total amount of each unit. For example in the number *3247*, 32 hundreds or 324 tens is easier to visualize when the number is written as 3247 as opposed to 3,247. In Grade 3 students understand 324 as 324 ones, 32 tens 4 ones or 3 hundreds 2 tens 4 ones. This flexible thinking allows for seeing simplifying short cuts. (E.g., When solving 3247 − 623, many students decompose 3 thousands rather than subtracting 6 hundreds from 32 hundreds. They might also solve thinking, 32 hundreds − 6 hundreds + 47 ones − 23 ones is 26 hundreds and 24 ones or 2624.)

NYS COMMON CORE MATHEMATICS CURRICULUM

Name __Jack_____   Date _____

1. Rewrite the following numbers including commas where appropriate:

a. 1234 1,234   b. 12345 12,345   c. 123456 123,456

d. 1234567 1,234,567   e. 12345678901 12,345,678,901

2. Complete the following chart:

Expression	Standard Form
5 tens + 5 tens	100
3 hundreds + 7 hundreds	1,000
400 thousands + 600 thousands	1,000,000
8 thousands + 4 thousands	12,000

3. Represent each addend with number disks in the place value chart. Show the composition of larger units from 10 smaller units. Write the sum in standard form.

a. 4 thousands + 11 hundreds = __5,100__

millions	hundred thousands	ten thousands	thousands	hundreds	tens	ones

b. 24 ten thousands + 11 thousands = __251,000__

millions	hundred thousands	ten thousands	thousands	hundreds	tens	ones

COMMON CORE   Lesson 3: Name numbers within one million by building understanding of the place value chart and placement of commas for naming base-thousand units.   engage^ny   1.A.8

© 2012 Common Core, Inc. All rights reserved. commoncore.org   Date: 4/27/13

COMMON CORE™

Lesson 3: Name numbers within 1 million by building understanding of the place value chart and placement of commas for naming base thousand units.

Date: 6/28/13

1.A.32

Exit Ticket (3 minutes)

After the Student Debrief, instruct students to complete
the Exit Ticket. A review of their work will help you assess
the students' understanding of the concepts that were
presented in the lesson today and plan more effectively
for future lessons. You may read the questions aloud to
the students.

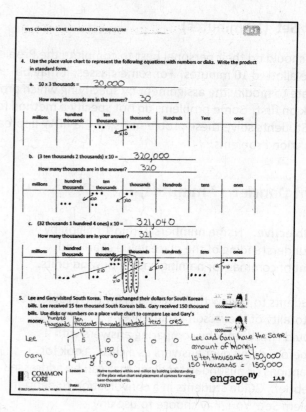

COMMON CORE™

Lesson 3:

Date:

Name numbers within 1 million by building understanding
of the place value chart and placement of commas for naming
base thousand units.
6/28/13

1.A.33

A   # Correct _____

Multiply.

1	1 x 3 =		23	10 x 3 =	
2	3 x 1 =		24	9 x 3 =	
3	2 x 3 =		25	4 x 3 =	
4	3 x 2 =		26	8 x 3 =	
5	3 x 3 =		27	5 x 3 =	
6	4 x 3 =		28	7 x 3 =	
7	3 x 4 =		29	6 x 3 =	
8	5 x 3 =		30	3 x 10 =	
9	3 x 5 =		31	3 x 5 =	
10	6 x 3 =		32	3 x 6 =	
11	3 x 6 =		33	3 x 1 =	
12	7 x 3 =		34	3 x 9 =	
13	3 x 7 =		35	3 x 4 =	
14	8 x 3 =		36	3 x 3 =	
15	3 x 8 =		37	3 x 2 =	
16	9 x 3 =		38	3 x 7 =	
17	3 x 9 =		39	3 x 8 =	
18	10 x 3 =		40	11 x 3 =	
19	3 x 10 =		41	3 x 11 =	
20	3 x 3 =		42	12 x 3 =	
21	1 x 3 =		43	3 x 13 =	
22	2 x 3 =		44	13 x 3 =	

© Bill Davidson

Lesson 3:   Name numbers within 1 million by building understanding
               of the place value chart and placement of commas for naming
Date: base thousand units.
               6/28/13

1.A.34

B

Multiply.

Improvement _____   # Correct _____

1	3 x 1 =		23	9 x 3 =	
2	1 x 3 =		24	3 x 3 =	
3	3 x 2 =		25	8 x 3 =	
4	2 x 3 =		26	4 x 3 =	
5	3 x 3 =		27	7 x 3 =	
6	3 x 4 =		28	5 x 3 =	
7	4 x 3 =		29	6 x 3 =	
8	3 x 5 =		30	3 x 5 =	
9	5 x 3 =		31	3 x 10 =	
10	3 x 6 =		32	3 x 1 =	
11	6 x 3 =		33	3 x 6 =	
12	3 x 7 =		34	3 x 4 =	
13	7 x 3 =		35	3 x 9 =	
14	3 x 8 =		36	3 x 2 =	
15	8 x 3 =		37	3 x 7 =	
16	3 x 9 =		38	3 x 3 =	
17	9 x 3 =		39	3 x 8 =	
18	3 x 10 =		40	11 x 3 =	
19	10 x 3 =		41	3 x 11 =	
20	1 x 3 =		42	13 x 3 =	
21	10 x 3 =		43	3 x 13 =	
22	2 x 3 =		44	12 x 3 =	

© Bill Davidson

Lesson 3:

Date:

Name numbers within 1 million by building understanding
of the place value chart and placement of commas for naming
base thousand units.

6/28/13

Name _____   Date _____

1. Rewrite the following numbers including commas where appropriate:

    a. 1234 _____.   b. 12345 _____   c. 123456 _____

    d. 1234567 _____   e. 12345678901 _____

2. Complete the following chart:

Expression	Standard Form
5 tens + 5 tens	
3 hundreds + 7 hundreds	
400 thousands + 600 thousands	
8 thousands + 4 thousands	

3. Represent each addend with number disks in the place value chart. Show the composition of larger units from 10 smaller units. Write the sum in standard form.

    a.   4 thousands + 11 hundreds = _____

millions	hundred thousands	ten thousands	thousands	hundreds	tens	ones

    b.   24 ten thousands + 11 thousands = _____

millions	hundred thousands	ten thousands	thousands	hundreds	tens	ones

Lesson 3:   Name numbers within 1 million by building understanding
             of the place value chart and placement of commas for naming
Date: base thousand units.
             6/28/13

1.A.36

4. Use the place value chart to represent the following equations with numbers or disks. Write the product in standard form.

    a. 10 x 3 thousands = _____

        How many thousands are in the answer? _____

millions	hundred thousands	ten thousands	thousands	hundreds	tens	ones

    b. (3 ten thousands 2 thousands) x 10 = _____

        How many thousands are in the answer? _____

millions	hundred thousands	ten thousands	thousands	hundreds	tens	ones

    c. (32 thousands 1 hundred 4 ones) x 10 = _____

        How many thousands are in your answer? _____

millions	hundred thousands	ten thousands	thousands	hundreds	tens	ones

5. Lee and Gary visited South Korea. They exchanged their dollars for South Korean bills. Lee received 15 ten thousand South Korean bills. Gary received 150 thousand bills. Use disks or numbers on a place value chart to compare Lee and Gary's money.

COMMON CORE™   **Lesson 3:**   Name numbers within 1 million by building understanding of the place value chart and placement of commas for naming base thousand units.   1.A.37

Date: 6/28/13

© 2013 Common Core, Inc. All rights reserved. commoncore.org

Name _____   Date _____

1. In the spaces provided, rewrite the following units as digits. Be sure to place commas where appropriate.

    a. 9 thousands, 3 hundreds, 4 ones _____

    b. 6 ten thousands, 2 thousands, 7 hundreds, 8 tens, 9 ones _____

    c. 1 hundred thousand, 8 thousands, 9 hundreds, 5 tens, 3 ones _____

2. Use the place value chart to write 26 thousands and 13 hundreds using digits.

millions	hundred thousands	ten thousands	thousands	hundreds	tens	ones

    How many thousands are in your answer? _____

Lesson 3:   Name numbers within 1 million by building understanding
                of the place value chart and placement of commas for naming
Date: base thousand units.
                6/28/13

© 2013 Common Core, Inc. All rights reserved. commoncore.org

1.A.38

Name _____   Date _____

1. Rewrite the following numbers including commas where appropriate:

   a. 4321 _____   b. 54321   _____

   c. 224466 _____   d. 2224466   _____

   e. 10010011001 _____

2. Complete the following chart:

Expression	Unit Form (Use the largest units possible.)	Standard Form
4 tens + 6 tens		
8 hundreds + 2 hundreds		
5 thousands + 7 thousands		

3. Represent each addend with number disks in the place value chart. Show the composition of larger units from 10 smaller units. Write the sum in standard form.

   a.   2 thousands + 12 hundreds = _____

millions	hundred thousands	ten thousands	thousands	hundreds	tens	ones

   b.   14 ten thousands + 12 thousands = _____

millions	hundred thousands	ten thousands	thousands	hundreds	tens	ones

COMMON CORE™   Lesson 3:   Name numbers within 1 million by building understanding
of the place value chart and placement of commas for naming
base thousand units.

Date: 6/28/13

1.A.39

4. Use the place value chart to represent the following equations with numbers or disks. Write the product in standard form.

a. 10 x 5 thousands = _____

How many thousands are in the answer? _____

millions	hundred thousands	ten thousands	thousands	hundreds	tens	ones

b. (4 ten thousands 4 thousands) x 10 = _____

How many thousands are in the answer? _____

millions	hundred thousands	ten thousands	thousands	hundreds	tens	ones

c. (27 thousands 3 hundreds 5 ones) x 10 = _____

How many thousands are in your answer? _____

millions	hundred thousands	ten thousands	thousands	hundreds	tens	ones

5. A large grocery store received an order of 2 thousand apples. A neighboring school received an order of 20 boxes of apples with 100 apples in each. Use disks or numbers on a place value chart to compare the number of apples received by the school and the number of apples received by the grocery store.

Lesson 3:   Name numbers within 1 million by building understanding
              of the place value chart and placement of commas for naming
Date: base thousand units.
              6/28/13

Lesson 4

Objective: Read and write multi-digit numbers using base ten numerals, number names, and expanded form.

Suggested Lesson Structure

■ Fluency Practice	(13 minutes)
■ Application Problem	(6 minutes)
■ Concept Development	(26 minutes)
■ Student Debrief	(15 minutes)
Total Time	**(60 minutes)**

Fluency Practice (13 minutes)

- Skip-Counting **3.OA.4–7**   (3 minutes)
- Place Value **4.NBT.2**   (2 minutes)
- Numbers Expressed in Different Base Units **4.NBT.1**   (8 minutes)

Skip-Counting (3 minutes)

Note: Practicing skip-counting on the number line builds a foundation for accessing higher order concepts throughout the year.

Direct students to skip-count by fours forward and backward to 48 focusing on transitions crossing the ten.

Place Value (2 minutes)

Materials: (S) Personal white boards, place value chart to the
              hundred thousands

Note: Reviewing and practicing place value skills in isolation will prepare students for success in writing multi-digit numbers in expanded form.

   T: Show 5 hundred thousands in number disks and write
       the number below it on the place value chart.

Students draw 5 hundred thousands disks, write 5 at the bottom of the ten thousands column and 0 in each column to the right of it. (Draw to correct student misunderstanding.)

NOTES ON MULTIPLE MEANS OF REPRESENTATION:

Place value fluency practices support language acquisition as it couples meaningful visuals with valuable practice speaking the standard and unit form of numbers to 1 million.

Lesson 4:	Read and write multi-digit numbers using base ten numerals, number names, and expanded form.	1.A.41
Date:	6/28/13	

© 2013 Common Core, Inc. All rights reserved. commoncore.org

T: Say the number in unit form.

S: 5 hundred thousands.

T: Say it in standard form 500,000.

Continue for the following possible sequence: 5 hundred thousands 3 ten thousands, 5 hundred thousands 3 hundreds, 5 ten thousands 3 hundreds, 1 hundred thousand 3 hundreds 5 tens, 4 hundred thousands, 2 ten thousands, 5 tens, 3 ones.

Numbers Expressed in Different Base Units (8 minutes)

Materials: (S) Personal white boards, place value chart to the millions

Note: This fluency will prepare students for success in writing multi-digit numbers in expanded form.

Base Hundred Units

T: (Project 3 hundreds = _____.) Say the number in standard form.

S: 300.

Continue with a suggested sequence of 9 hundreds, 10 hundreds, 19 hundreds, 21 hundreds, 33 hundreds, 30 hundreds, 100 hundreds, 200 hundreds, 500 hundreds, 530 hundreds, 537 hundreds, and 864 hundreds.

Base Thousand Units

T: (Project 5 thousands = _____.) Say the number in standard form.

S: 5000.

Continue with a suggested sequence of 9 thousands, 10 thousands, 20 thousands, 100 thousands, 220 thousands, and 347 thousands.

Base Ten Thousand Units

T: (Project 7 ten thousands = _____.) Say the number in standard form.

S: 70,000.

Continue with a suggested sequence of 9 ten thousands, 10 ten thousands, 12 ten thousands, 19 ten thousands, 20 ten thousands, 30 ten thousands, 80 ten thousands, 800 ten thousands, 817 ten thousands, and 438 ten thousands.

Base Hundred Thousand Units

T: (Project 3 hundred thousands = _____.) Say the number in standard form.

S: 300,000.

Continue with a suggested sequence of 6 hundred thousands, 9 hundred thousands, 10 hundred thousands, 20 hundred thousands, 70 hundred thousands, 71 hundred thousands, 75 hundred thousands, and 43 hundred thousands.

Application Problem (6 minutes)

There are about forty-one thousand Asian elephants and about four hundred seventy thousand African elephants left in the world. About how many Asian and African elephants are left in total?

Note: This application problem builds on the content of the previous lesson, requiring students to name base thousand units. It also builds from **3.NBT.2** (fluently add and subtract within 1000). Assist students by asking them to add using unit names (similar to the example), not the entire numbers as digits.

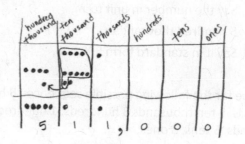

41 thousand Asian
+ 470 thousand African
511 thousand elephants

Concept Development (26 minutes)

Materials: (S) Personal white boards

Problem 1

Write a four-digit number in expanded form.

T: On your place value chart write the following number: 1,708.

T: What is the value of the 1?

S: 1,000.

T: (Write 1,000 under the thousands place.) What is the value of the 7?

S: 700. (Record 700 under the hundreds.)

T: What value does zero have?

S: Zero.

T: What is the value of 8?

S: 8. (Record 8.)

T: What is the value of 1,000 and 700 and 8?

S: 1,708.

T: So, 1,708 is the same as 1,000 plus 700 plus 8.

T: Write a number sentence to show that equation.

S: 1,000 + 700 + 8 = 1,708.

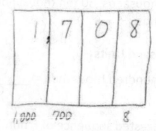

NOTES ON MULTIPLE MEANS OF ACTION AND EXPRESSION:

Scaffold student composition of number words with the following of options:

- Provide individual cards with number words that can be easily copied.
- Allow students to abbreviate number words.
- Set individual goals for writing number words.
- Allow ELLs their language of choice for expressing number words.

COMMON CORE | Lesson 4: Read and write multi-digit numbers using base ten numerals, number names, and expanded form.

Date: 6/28/13

1.A.43

Problem 2

Write a five-digit number in word form and expanded form.

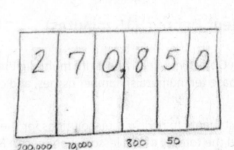

T: Now erase your values and write this number: 27,085.

T: Show the value of each digit at the bottom of your place value chart.

S: 20,000, 7,000, 80, and 5.

T: Why is there no term representing the hundreds?

S: Zero stands for nothing. → Zero added to a number doesn't change the value.

T: With your partner write an addition sentence.

S: 20,000 + 7,000 + 80 + 5 = 27,085.

T: Now, read the expanded sentence with me.

S: Twenty thousand plus seven thousand plus eighty plus five equals twenty-seven thousand, eighty-five.

T: (Write the number as you speak.) You said "twenty-seven thousand, eighty five."

T: What do you notice about where I placed a comma in both the standard form and word form?

S: It is placed after 27 to separate the thousands in both the standard form and word form.

Problem 3

Transcribe a number in word form to standard and expanded form.

Display two hundred seventy thousand, eight hundred fifty.

T: Read this number. (Students read.) Tell your partner how you can match the word form to the standard form?

S: Everything you say, you should write in words. → The comma helps to separate the numbers in the thousands from the numbers in the hundreds, tens, and ones.

T: Write this number in your place value chart. Now, write this number in expanded form. Tell your partner your equation.

S: 200,000 + 70,000 + 800 + 50 equals 270,850.

Repeat with sixty-four thousand, three.

Lesson 4:   Read and write multi-digit numbers using base ten numerals, number names, and expanded form.

Date: 6/28/13

Problem 4

Convert a number in expanded form to word and standard form.

Display 700,000 + 8,000 + 500 + 70 + 3

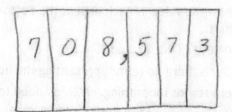

MP.3

T: Read this number statement. (Students read.) On your own, write this number in your place value chart.

T: My sum is 78,573. Compare your sum with mine.

S: Your 7 is in the wrong place. → The value of the 7 is 700,000. Your 7 has a value of 70,000.

T: Read this number in standard form with me.

S: Seven hundred eight thousand, five hundred seventy-three.

T: Write this number in words. Remember to check for correct use of commas and hyphens.

Repeat with 500,000 + 30,000 + 10 + 3

Problem Set (10 minutes)

Students should do their personal best to complete the Problem Set within the allotted 10 minutes. For some classes, it may be appropriate to modify the assignment by specifying which problems they work on first. Some problems do not specify a method for solving. Students solve these problems using the RDW approach used for Application Problems.

Student Debrief (15 minutes)

Lesson Objective: Read and write multi-digit numbers using base ten numerals, number names, and expanded form.

Invite students to review their solutions for the Problem Set and the totality of the lesson experience. They should check work by comparing answers with a partner before going over answers as a class. Look for misconceptions or misunderstandings that can be addressed in the Debrief. Guide students in a conversation to debrief the Problem Set. You may choose to use any combination of the questions below to lead the discussion.

- Compare the numbers in Problems 1 and 2. What do you notice?

- As you completed the chart on Page 2, what number words were tricky to write? Which number words can be confused with other number words? Why? What strategies did you use to spell number words?

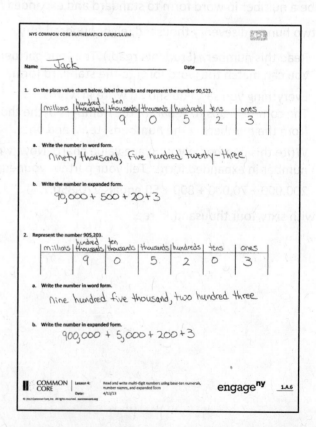

COMMON CORE™   Lesson 4:   Read and write multi-digit numbers using base ten numerals, number names, and expanded form.
Date: 6/28/13

© 2013 Common Core, Inc. All rights reserved. commoncore.org   1.A.45

- Timothy and his dad read a number word in two ways. What other numbers can be read more than one way? Which way of reading a number best helps you solve? When?

- Two students discussed the importance of zero. Nate said that zero is not important, while Jill said that zero is extremely important. Who is right? Why do you think so?

- What role can zero play in a number?

- How is expanded form related to the standard form of a number?

- When might you use expanded form to solve?

Exit Ticket (3 minutes)

After the Student Debrief, instruct students to complete the Exit Ticket. A review of their work will help you assess the students' understanding of the concepts that were presented in the lesson today and plan more effectively for future lessons. You may read the questions aloud to the students.

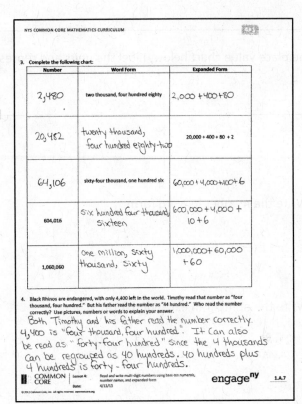

NYS COMMON CORE MATHEMATICS CURRICULUM

3. Complete the following chart:

Number	Word Form	Expanded Form
2,480	two thousand, four hundred eighty	2,000 + 400 + 80
20,482	twenty thousand, four hundred eighty-two	20,000 + 400 + 80 + 2
64,106	sixty-four thousand, one hundred six	60,000 + 4,000 + 100 + 6
604,016	Six hundred four thousand, sixteen	600,000 + 4,000 + 10 + 6
1,060,060	One million, sixty thousand, sixty	1,000,000 + 60,000 + 60

4. Black Rhinos are endangered, with only 4,400 left in the world. Timothy read that number as "four thousand, four hundred." But his father read the number as "44 hundred." Who read the number correctly? Use pictures, numbers or words to explain your answer.

Both Timothy and his father read the number correctly. 4,400 is "four thousand, four hundred". It can also be read as "forty-four hundred" since the 4 thousands can be regrouped as 40 hundreds. 40 hundreds plus 4 hundreds is forty-four hundreds.

COMMON CORE | Lesson 4: | Read and write multi-digit numbers using base-ten numerals, number names, and expanded form.   engage^ny   1.A.7
Date: | 4/13/13

© 2012 Common Core, Inc. All rights reserved. commoncore.org

COMMON CORE™   Lesson 4:   Read and write multi-digit numbers using base ten numerals, number names, and expanded form.   1.A.46
Date: 6/28/13

© 2013 Common Core, Inc. All rights reserved. commoncore.org

Name _____   Date _____

1. On the place value chart below, label the units and represent the number 90,523.

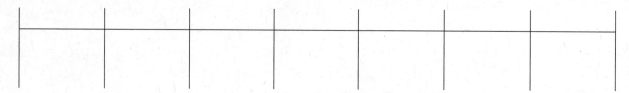

    a. Write the number in word form.

    b. Write the number in expanded form.

2. Represent the number 905,203.

    a. Write the number in word form.

    b. Write the number in expanded form.

COMMON CORE™

Lesson 4:   Read and write multi-digit numbers using base ten numerals, number
            names, and expanded form.
Date: 6/28/13

1.A.47

3. Complete the following chart:

Number	Word Form	Expanded Form
	two thousand, four hundred eighty	
		20,000 + 400 + 80 + 2
	sixty-four thousand, one hundred six	
604,016		
1,060,060		

4. Black Rhinos are endangered, with only 4,400 left in the world. Timothy read that number as "four thousand, four hundred." But his father read the number as "44 hundred." Who read the number correctly? Use pictures, numbers, or words to explain your answer.

Name _____   Date _____

1. Use the place value chart below to complete the following:

a. Label the units on the chart.

b. Write the number 800,000 + 6,000 + 300 + 2 in the place value chart.

c. Write the number in word form.

2. Write one hundred sixty thousand, five hundred eighty-two in expanded form.

Lesson 4:   Read and write multi-digit numbers using base ten numerals, number names, and expanded form.

Date: 6/28/13

1.A.49

Name _____   Date _____

1. On the place value chart below, label the units and represent the number 50,679.

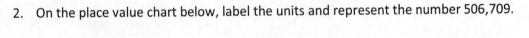

    a. Write the number in word form.

    b. Write the number in expanded form.

2. On the place value chart below, label the units and represent the number 506,709.

    a. Write the number in word form.

    b. Write the number in expanded form.

COMMON CORE™   Lesson 4:   Read and write multi-digit numbers using base ten numerals, number
                                    names, and expanded form.   1.A.50
                     Date: 6/28/13

3. Complete the following chart:

Number	Word Form	Expanded Form
	five thousand, three hundred seventy	
		50,000 + 300 + 70 + 2
	thirty-nine thousand, seven hundred one	
309,017		
1,070,070		

4. Use pictures, numbers, and words to explain another way to say "sixty-five hundred."

COMMON CORE™

Lesson 4: Read and write multi-digit numbers using base ten numerals, number names, and expanded form.

Date: 6/28/13

1.A.51

© 2013 Common Core, Inc. All rights reserved. commoncore.org

Topic B

Comparing Multi-Digit Whole Numbers

4.NBT.2

Focus Standard:	4.NBT.2	Read and write multi-digit whole numbers using base-ten numerals, number names, and expanded form. Compare two multi-digit numbers based on meanings of the digits in each place, using >, =, and < symbols to record the results of comparisons.
Instructional Days:	2	
Coherence -Links from:	G2–M3	Place Value, Counting, and Comparison of Numbers to 1000
-Links to:	G5–M1	Place Value and Decimal Fractions

In Topic B, students use place value to compare whole numbers. Initially using the place value chart, students will compare the value of each digit to surmise which number is of greater value. Moving away from dependency on models and towards fluency with numbers, students compare numbers by observing across the entire number and noticing value differences. For example, in comparing 12,566 to 19,534, it is evident that 19 thousand is greater than 12 thousand because of the meaning of the digits in the thousands. Additionally, students continue with number fluency by finding what is 1, 10, or 100 thousand more or less than a given number.

A Teaching Sequence Towards Mastery of Comparing Multi-Digit Whole Numbers
Objective 1: Compare numbers based on meanings of the digits, using >, <, or = to record the comparison.   (Lesson 5)
Objective 2: Find 1, 10, and 100 thousand more and less than a given number.   (Lesson 6)

Lesson 5

Objective: Compare numbers based on meanings of the digits, using >, <, or = to record the comparison.

Suggested Lesson Structure

■ Fluency Practice   (14 minutes)
▨ Application Problem   (6 minutes)
▨ Concept Development   (30 minutes)
■ Student Debrief   (10 minutes)
  Total Time   **(60 minutes)**

Fluency Practice (14 minutes)

- Multiply by 4 **3.OA.7**   (10 minutes)
- Unit Skip-Counting **4.NBT.1**   (2 minutes)
- Place Value **4.NBT.2**   (2 minutes)

Sprint: Multiply by 4 (10 minutes)

Materials: (S) Multiply by 4 Sprint

Note: This fluency will review a foundational third grade standard that will help students learn standard **4.NBT.5**.

Unit Skip-Counting (2 minutes)

Note: This fluency will apply skip-counting fluency that was built during the first four lessons and apply it to the multiplying by ten lessons.

    T: Count by twos.
    S: 2, 4, 6, 8, 10, 12, 14, 16, 18, 20.
    T: Now count by 2 tens. Stop counting and raise your hand when you see me raise my hand.
    S: 2 tens, 4 tens, 6 tens. (Raise hand.)

Students raise hand.

    T: Say the number in standard form.
    S: 60.

Continue stopping the students at 12 tens, 16 tens, and 20 tens.

Lesson 5:	Compare numbers based on meanings of the digits, using >, <, or = to record the comparison.	
Date:	6/28/13	1.B.2

Repeat the process for threes and three ten thousands.

Place Value (2 minutes)

Note: Reviewing and practicing place value skills in isolation will prepare students for success in comparing numbers during the lesson.

T: (Write 3,487.) Say the number.

S: 3,487.

T: What digit is in the tens place?

S: 8.

T: (Underline 8.) What's the value of the 8?

S: 80.

T: State the value of the 3.

S: 3,000.

T: 4?

S: 400.

Repeat for the following possible sequence: 59,607; 287,493; and 7,142,952.

Application Problem (6 minutes)

Draw and label the units on the place value chart. Use each of the following digits (9, 8, 7, 3, 1, 0) once to create a number that is between 7 hundred thousand and 9 hundred thousand. Write the number you created in word form.

Bonus: Create 2 more numbers following the same directions as above.

Note: This application problem builds on the content of the previous lesson, requiring students to read and write multi-digit numbers in expanded, word, and unit forms.

hundred thousands	ten thousands	thousands	hundreds	tens	ones
8	3	7	9	1	0

eight hundred thirty-seven thousand, nine hundred ten

Concept Development (30 minutes)

Materials: (S) Place value boards and markers (or place value disks)

Problem 1

Comparing two numbers with the same largest unit.

Display: 3,010 ◯ 2,040

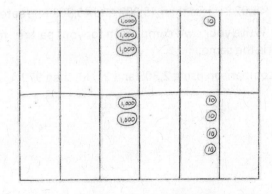

COMMON CORE

Lesson 5:   Compare numbers based on meanings of the digits,
             using >, <, or = to record the comparison.
Date: 6/28/13

1.B.3

© 2013 Common Core, Inc. All rights reserved. commoncore.org

T: Let's compare two numbers. Say the standard form to your partner and model each number on your place value board.

S: Three thousand, ten. Two thousand, forty.

T: What is the name of the unit with the greatest value?

S: Thousands.

T: Compare the value of the thousands.

S: 3 thousand is greater than 2 thousand. → 2 thousand is less than 3 thousand.

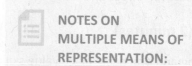

NOTES ON MULTIPLE MEANS OF REPRESENTATION:

Provide sentence frames for students to refer to when using comparative statements.

T: Tell your partner what would happen if we only compared tens rather than the unit with the greatest value.

S: We would say that 2,040 is greater than 3,010 but that isn't right. → The number with more of the largest unit being compared is greater. → We don't need to compare the tens because the thousands are different.

T: Thousands are our largest unit. 3 thousand is greater than 2 thousand so 3,010 is greater than 2,040. (Write the comparison symbol ">" in the circle.) Write this comparison statement on your board and say it to your partner in two different ways.

S: 3,010 is greater than 2,040 and 2,040 is less than 3,010. (3,010 > 2,040)

Problem 2

Comparing two numbers with an equal amount of the largest units.

Display: 43,021 45,302

T: Model and read each number. How is this comparison different from our first comparison?

S: Before, our largest unit was thousands, now our largest unit is ten thousands. → In this comparison, both numbers have the same number of ten thousands.

T: If the digits of the largest unit are equal, how do we compare?

S: We compare the thousands. → We compare the next largest unit. → We compare the digit one place to the right.

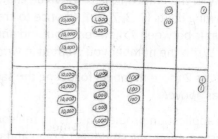

T: Write your comparison statement on your board. (Students write.) Say the comparison statement in two ways.

S: 43,021 is less than 45,302 and 45,302 is greater than 43,021. (43,021 < 45,302)

T: Write your own comparison for your partner to solve. Create a comparison in which the largest unit is the same.

Repeat comparison using 2,305 and 2,530, then 970,461 and 907,641.

COMMON CORE™

Lesson 5:   Compare numbers based on meanings of the digits, using >, <, or = to record the comparison.
Date: 6/28/13

1.B.4

Problem 3

Comparing values of multiple numbers using a place value chart.

T: Write the following numbers in your place value chart. Whisper the value of each digit as you do so.

Model these three numbers in your place value chart as numerals.

    32,434   32,644   32,534

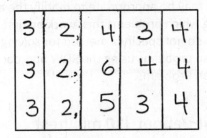

T: When you compare the value of these three numbers, what do you notice?

S: All three numbers have 3 ten thousands. → All three numbers have 2 thousands. → We can compare the hundreds because they are different.

T: Which number has the greatest value?

S: 32,644.

T: Tell your partner which number has the least value and how you know.

S: 32,434 is the smallest of the three numbers because it has the least number of hundreds.

T: Arrange the numbers from greatest to least. Use comparison symbols to express the relationships of the numbers.

S: 32,644 > 32,534 > 32,434

Problem 4

Comparing numbers in different number forms.

Display: Compare 700,000 + 30,000 + 20 + 8 and 735,008

T: Discuss with your partner how to solve this comparison and write your comparison.

S: I will write the numerals in my place value chart to compare. → Draw disks for each number. → I'll write the first number in standard form, then compare.

S: 730,028 < 735,008

T: Tell your partner which units you compared and why.

S: I compared thousands because the larger units were the same. 5 thousands are greater than zero thousands, so 735,008 is greater than 730,028.

Repeat with 4 hundred thousands, 8 thousands, and 9 tens, and 40,000 + 8,000 + 90.

NOTES ON MULTIPLE MEANS FOR ACTION AND EXPRESSION:

For students who have difficulty converting numbers from expanded form into standard form, demonstrate, using a place value chart, how each number can be represented and then how the numbers can be added together. Alternatively, use place value cards to allow students to see the value of each digit that composes a number. The cards help students to be able to manipulate and visually display the expanded form of a number and the standard form of a number.

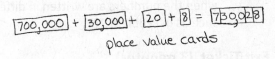

place value cards

Lesson 5:   Compare numbers based on meanings of the digits, using >, <, or = to record the comparison.

Date: 6/28/13

1.B.5

Problem Set (10 minutes)

Students should do their personal best to complete the Problem Set within the allotted 10 minutes. For some classes, it may be appropriate to modify the assignment by specifying which problems they work on first. Some problems do not specify a method for solving. Students solve these problems using the RDW approach used for Application Problems.

Student Debrief (10 minutes)

Lesson Objective: Compare numbers based on meanings of the digits, using >, <, or = to record the comparison.

Invite students to review their solutions for the Problem Set and the totality of the lesson experience. They should check work by comparing answers with a partner before going over answers as a class. Look for misconceptions or misunderstandings that can be addressed in the Debrief. Guide students in a conversation to debrief the Problem Set. You may choose to use any combination of the questions below to lead the discussion.

- Which is more helpful to you: line up digits or line up number disks in a place value chart to compare numbers?
- How is comparing numbers in Problem 1(a) different from Problem 1(b)?
- How does your understanding of place value help to compare and order numbers?
- How can ordering numbers apply to real life?
- What challenges arise in comparing numbers when the numbers are written in different forms, such as in Problem 2?

Exit Ticket (3 minutes)

After the Student Debrief, instruct students to complete the Exit Ticket. A review of their work will help you assess the students' understanding of the concepts that were presented in the lesson today and plan more effectively for future lessons. You may read the questions aloud to the students.

COMMON CORE

Lesson 5:

Date:

Compare numbers based on meanings of the digits, using >, <, or = to record the comparison.
6/28/13

1.B.6

© 2013 Common Core, Inc. All rights reserved. **commoncore.org**

A

Multiply.   # Correct _____

1	1 x 4 =		23	10 x 4 =	
2	4 x 1 =		24	9 x 4 =	
3	2 x 4 =		25	4 x 4 =	
4	4 x 2 =		26	8 x 4 =	
5	3 x 4 =		27	4 x 3 =	
6	4 x 3 =		28	7 x 4 =	
7	4 x 4 =		29	6 x 4 =	
8	5 x 4 =		30	4 x 10 =	
9	4 x 5 =		31	4 x 5 =	
10	6 x 4 =		32	4 x 6 =	
11	4 x 6 =		33	4 x 1 =	
12	7 x 4 =		34	4 x 9 =	
13	4 x 7 =		35	4 x 4 =	
14	8 x 4 =		36	4 x 3 =	
15	4 x 8 =		37	4 x 2 =	
16	9 x 4 =		38	4 x 7 =	
17	4 x 9 =		39	4 x 8 =	
18	10 x 4 =		40	11 x 4 =	
19	4 x 10 =		41	4 x 11 =	
20	4 x 3 =		42	12 x 4 =	
21	1 x 4 =		43	4 x 12 =	
22	2 x 4 =		44	13 x 4 =	

© Bill Davidson

B

Improvement _____   # Correct _____

Multiply.

1	4 x 1 =		23	9 x 4 =	
2	1 x 4 =		24	3 x 4 =	
3	4 x 2 =		25	8 x 4 =	
4	2 x 4 =		26	4 x 4 =	
5	4 x 3 =		27	7 x 4 =	
6	3 x 4 =		28	5 x 4 =	
7	4 x 4 =		29	6 x 4 =	
8	4 x 5 =		30	4 x 5 =	
9	5 x 4 =		31	4 x 10 =	
10	4 x 6 =		32	4 x 1 =	
11	6 x 4 =		33	4 x 6 =	
12	4 x 7 =		34	4 x 4 =	
13	7 x 4 =		35	4 x 9 =	
14	4 x 8 =		36	4 x 2 =	
15	8 x 4 =		37	4 x 7 =	
16	4 x 9 =		38	4 x 3 =	
17	9 x 4 =		39	4 x 8 =	
18	4 x 10 =		40	11 x 4 =	
19	10 x 4 =		41	4 x 11 =	
20	1 x 4 =		42	12 x 4 =	
21	10 x 4 =		43	4 x 12 =	
22	2 x 4 =		44	13 x 4 =	

© Bill Davidson

Lesson 5:   Compare numbers based on meanings of the digits,
          using >, <, or = to record the comparison.
Date: 6/28/13

1.B.8

Name _____   Date _____

1. Label the units in the place value chart. Draw place value disks to represent each number in the place value chart. Use <, >, or = to compare the two numbers. Write the correct symbol in the circle.

   a.   600,015 ◯ 60,015

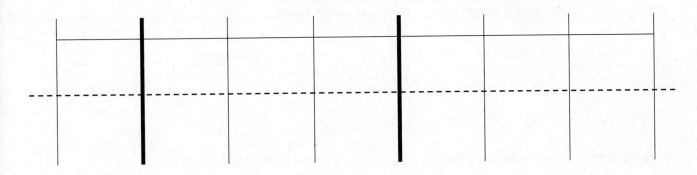

   b.   409,004 ◯ 440,002

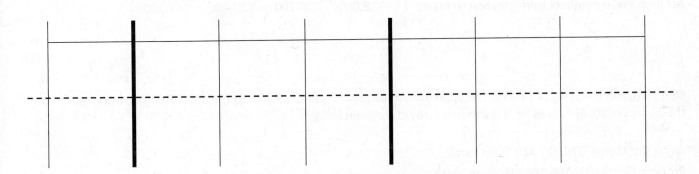

2. Compare the two numbers by using the symbols <, >, and =. Write the correct symbol in the circle.

   a. 342,001 ◯ 94,981

   b. 500,000 + 80,000 + 9,000 + 100 ◯ five hundred eight thousand, nine hundred one

   c. 9 hundred thousands 8 thousands 9 hundreds 3 tens ◯ 908,930

   d. 9 hundreds 5 ten thousands 9 ones ◯ 6 ten thousands 5 hundreds 9 ones

| Lesson 5: | Compare numbers based on meanings of the digits, using >, <, or = to record the comparison. |
| Date: | 6/28/13 |

1.B.9

3. Use the information in the chart below to list the height in feet of each mountain from least to greatest. Then name the mountain that has the lowest elevation in feet.

Name of Mountain	Elevation in Feet (ft.)
Allen Mountain	4,347 ft.
Mount Marcy	5,343 ft.
Mount Haystack	4,960 ft.
Slide Mountain	4,180 ft.

4. Arrange these numbers from least to greatest: 8,002   2,080   820   2,008   8,200

5. Arrange these numbers from greatest to least: 728,000   708,200   720,800   87,300

6. One astronomical unit, or 1 AU, is the approximate distance from the earth to the sun. The following are the approximate distances from earth to nearby stars given in AUs:

Alpha Centauri is 275,725 AUs from earth.

Proxima Centauri is 268,269 AUs from earth.

Epsilon Eridani is 665,282 AUs from earth.

Barnard's Star is 377,098 AUs from earth.

Sirius is 542,774 AUs from earth.

List the names of the stars and their distances in AUs in order from closest to farthest from earth.

Name _____   Date _____

1. Four friends were playing a game. Use the information in the table below to order the number of points each player earned from least to greatest. Then name the person who won the game.

Player Name	Points Earned
Amy	2,398 points
Bonnie	2,976 points
Jeff	2,709 points
Rick	2,699 points

2. Use each of the digits 5, 4, 3, 2, 1 exactly once to create two different five-digit numbers.

   a. Write each number on the line and compare the two numbers by using the symbols < or >.
      Write the correct symbol in the circle.

   _____ ◯ _____

   b. Use words to write a comparison statement for the problem above.

COMMON CORE | Lesson 5:   Compare numbers based on meanings of the digits,   1.B.11
                                using >, <, or = to record the comparison.
                   | Date: 6/28/13

© 2013 Common Core, Inc. All rights reserved. commoncore.org

Name _____   Date _____

1. Label the units in the place value chart. Draw place value disks to represent each number in the place value chart. Use <, >, or = to compare the two numbers. Write the correct symbol in the circle.

   a.   909,013   90,013

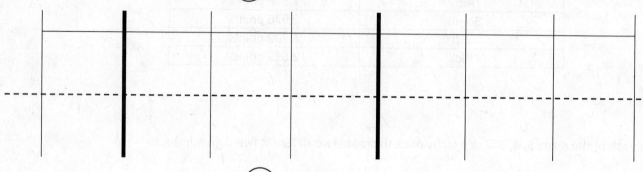

   b.   210,005   220,005

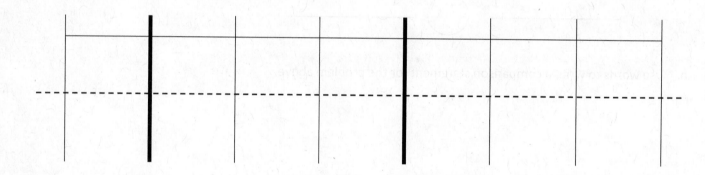

2. Compare the two numbers by using the symbols <, >, and =. Write the correct symbol in the circle.

   a. 501,107   89,171

   b. 300,000 + 50,000 + 1,000 + 800  six hundred five thousand, nine hundred eight

   c. 3 hundred thousands 3 thousands 8 hundreds 4 tens 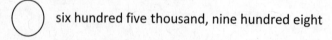 303,840

   d. 5 hundreds 6 ten thousands 2 ones   3 ten thousands 5 hundreds 1 one

3. Use the information in the chart below to list the height in feet of each skyscraper from least to greatest. Then name the tallest skyscraper.

Name of Skyscraper	Height of Skyscraper (ft.)
Willis Tower	1,450
Freedom Tower	1,776
Taipei 101	1,670
Petronas Towers	1,483

4. Arrange these numbers from least to greatest: 7,550   5,070   750   5,007   7,505

5. Arrange these numbers from greatest to least: 426,000   406,200   640,020   46,600

6. The area of the 50 states can be measured in square miles (sq. miles).

California is 158,648 sq. miles. Nevada is 110,567 sq. miles. Arizona is 114,007 sq. miles.
Texas is 266,874 sq. miles. Montana is 147,047 sq. miles, and Alaska is 587,878 sq. miles.

Arrange the states listed by area from least to greatest.

Lesson 6

Objective: Find 1, 10, and 100 thousand more and less than a given number.

Suggested Lesson Structure

- ■ Fluency Practice   (12 minutes)
- ▦ Application Problem   (4 minutes)
- ▦ Concept Development   (33 minutes)
- ■ Student Debrief   (11 minutes)
- **Total Time**   **(60 minutes)**

Fluency Practice (12 minutes)

- ▪ Unit Skip Counting **4.NBT.1**   (3 minutes)
- ▪ Rename the Units **4.NBT.2**   (5 minutes)
- ▪ Compare Numbers **4.NBT.2**   (4 minutes)

Unit Skip-Counting (3 minutes)

Note: This fluency will apply skip-counting fluency to the multiplying by ten lessons.

- T: Count by threes.
- S: 3, 6, 9, 12, 15, 18, 21, 24, 27, 30.
- T: Now count by 3 ten thousands. Stop counting and raise your hand when you see me raise my hand.
- S: 3 ten thousands, 6 ten thousands, 9 ten thousands. (Raise hand.)

Students raise hand.

- T: Say the number in standard form.
- S: 90,000.

Continue stopping the students at 15 ten thousands, 21 ten thousands, and 30 ten thousands.

Repeat process for fours and 4 hundred thousands.

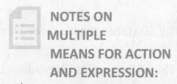

NOTES ON MULTIPLE MEANS FOR ACTION AND EXPRESSION:

Before directing the students to count by *3 ten thousands*, first direct them to count by *3 cats*. Then direct them to count by *3 hundreds*. Then bridge the directions to counting by *3 ten thousands*.

Rename the Units (5 minutes)

Note: This fluency applies students' place value skills in a new context that will help them better access the lesson's content.

Materials: (S) Personal white boards

    T: (Write 54,783.) Say the number.

    S: 54,783.

    T: How many thousands are in 54,783?

    S: 54 thousands.

    T: (Write 54,783 = _____ thousands ____ ones.) On your boards, fill-in the number sentence.

Students write 54,783 = 54 thousands 783 ones.

    T: How many ten thousands are in 54,783?

    S: 5 ten thousands.

    T: (Write 54,783 = _____ ten thousands ____ hundreds ____ ones.) On your white boards, fill-in the number sentence.

Students write 54,783 = 5 ten thousands 47 hundreds 83 ones. Follow the same process and sequence for 234,673.

Compare Numbers (4 minutes)

Materials: (S) Personal white boards

Note: This fluency will review comparing number concepts learned in Lesson 5.

    T: (Write 231,005 _____ 83,872.)

On your personal white boards, compare the numbers by writing the greater than, less than, or equal symbol.

Students write 231,005 > 83,872.

Repeat for possible sequence: 6 thousands 4 hundreds 9 tens; 5 ten thousands 4 hundreds 9 ones; and 8 hundred thousands 7 thousands 8 hundreds 2 tens _____ 807,820.

Application Problem (4 minutes)

Use the digits 5, 6, 8, 2, 4, and 1 to create two six-digit numbers. Be sure to use each of the digits within both numbers. Express the numbers in word form and use a comparison sign to show their relationship.

Note: This application problem builds on the content of the previous two lessons.

Example: 586,241   412,685
five hundred eighty-six thousand, two hundred forty-one   <
four hundred twelve thousand, six hundred eighty-five

COMMON CORE   Lesson 6:   Find 1, 10, and 100 thousand more and less than a given number.
                      Date: 6/28/13   1.B.15

Concept Development (33 minutes)

Materials: (T) Base ten disks: ones, tens, hundreds, and thousands (S) Personal white boards

Problem 1

Find 1 thousand more and 1 thousand less.

T: (Draw 2 thousand disks in the place value chart.) How many thousands do you count?

S: Two thousands.

T: What number is one thousand more? (Draw 1 more thousand.)

S: Three thousand.

T: (Write 3 thousand 112 ones.) Model this number with disks and write its expanded and standard form.

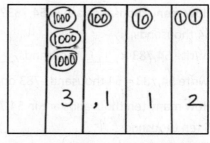

T: Draw 1 more unit of one thousand. What number is 1 thousand more than 3,112?

S: 4,112 is 1 thousand more than 3,112.

T: 1 thousand less than 3,112?

S: 2,112.

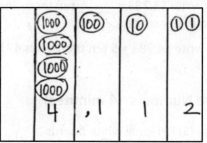

T: Draw 1 ten thousand disk. What number do you have now?

S: 14,112.

T: Show 1 less unit of 1 thousand. What number is 1 thousand less than 14,112?

S: 13,112.

T: 1 thousand more than 14,112?

S: 15,112.

T: Did the largest unit change? Discuss with your partner.

S: (Students discuss.)

T: Show 19,112. (Pause as they do so.) What is 1 thousand less? 1 thousand more than 19,112?

T: Did the largest unit change? Discuss with your partner.

S: (Students discuss.)

T: Show 199,465. (Pause as they do so.) What is 1 thousand less? 1 thousand more than 199,465?

T: Did the largest unit change? Discuss with your partner.

S: (Students discuss.)

MP.5

Lesson 6:   Find 1, 10, and 100 thousand more and less than a given number.
Date: 6/28/13

1.B.16

Problem 2

Find 10 thousand more and 10 thousand less.

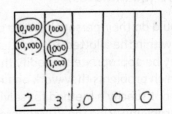

    T: Use numbers and disks to model 2 ten thousands 3 thousands. Read and write the expanded form.

    S: 20,000 + 3,000 = 23,000.

    T: What number is 10 thousand more than 2 ten thousands 3 thousands? Draw, read, and write the expanded form.

    S: 20,000 + 10,000 + 3,000 = 33,000.

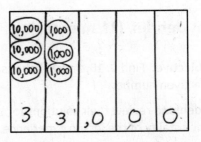

    T: (Display 100,000 + 30,000 + 4,000.) Use disks and numbers to model the sum. What number is 10 thousand more than 134,000? Say your answer as an addition sentence.

    S: 10,000 + 134,000 is 144,000.

    T: (Display 25,130 – 10,000.) What number is 10 thousand less than 25,130? Work with your partner to use numbers and disks to model the difference. Write and whisper to your partner an equation in unit form to verify your answer.

    S: 2 ten thousands 5 thousands 1 hundred 3 tens minus 1 ten thousand is 1 ten thousand 5 thousands 1 hundred 3 tens.

Problem 3

Find 100 thousand more and 100 thousand less.

    T: (Display 200,352.) Work with your partner to find the number that is 100 thousand more than 200,352. Write an equation to verify your answer.

    T: (Display 545,000 and 445,000 and 345,000.) Read these three numbers to your partner. Predict the next number in my pattern and explain your reasoning.

    S: I predict the next number will be 245,000. I notice the numbers decrease by 100,000. 345,000 minus 100,000 is 245,000. → I notice the hundred thousand units decreasing: 5 hundred thousands, 4 hundred thousands, 3 hundred thousands. I predict the next number will have 2 hundred thousands. I notice the other units do not change. So, the next number will be 2 hundred thousands 4 ten thousands 5 thousands.

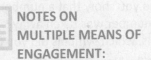

NOTES ON MULTIPLE MEANS OF ENGAGEMENT:

After students predict the next number in the pattern, ask students to create their own pattern using the strategy of one thousand more or less, ten thousand more or less, or one hundred thousand more or less. Then ask students to challenge their classmates to predict the next number in the pattern.

Problem Set (10 minutes)

Students should do their personal best to complete the Problem Set within the allotted 10 minutes. For some classes, it may be appropriate to modify the assignment by specifying which problems they work on first. Some problems do not specify a method for solving. Students solve these problems using the RDW approach used for Application Problems.

Student Debrief (11 minutes)

Lesson Objective: Find 1, 10, and 100 thousand more and less than a given number.

Invite students to review their solutions for the Problem Set and the totality of the lesson experience. They should check work by comparing answers with a partner before going over answers as a class. Look for misconceptions or misunderstandings that can be addressed in the Debrief. Guide students in a conversation to debrief the Problem Set. You may choose to use any combination of the questions below to lead the discussion.

- When drawing number disks in the Problem Set, how did you show that a number was added or that a number was taken away? If you used symbols, which symbols did you use?

- Look at Problem 2 In the Problem Set. How did you solve? Compare your method to your partner's. How else could you model?

- Why were Problems 3(e) and 3(f) more challenging than the rest? How did you use your place value knowledge to solve?

- Look at Problem 4. What strategy did you use to complete the pattern? How many ways can we model to solve? Which way is best? Why do you think so?

- Compare Problem 3 and Problem 4? Which was easier to solve? Why?

- How does your understanding of place value help you add or subtract 1,000, 10,000 and 100,000?

- What place value patterns have we discovered?

Lesson 6:   Find 1, 10, and 100 thousand more and less than a given number.
Date: 6/28/13

1.B.18

Exit Ticket (3 minutes)

After the Student Debrief, instruct students to complete the Exit Ticket. A review of their work will help you assess the students' understanding of the concepts that were presented in the lesson today and plan more effectively for future lessons. You may read the questions aloud to the students.

Lesson 6:   Find 1, 10, and 100 thousand more and less than a given number.
Date: 6/28/13

1.B.19

Name _____ Date _____

1. Label the place value chart. Use number disks to find the sum or difference. Write the answer in standard form on the line.

   a. 10,000 more than six hundred five thousand, four hundred, seventy-two is _____.

   b. 100 thousand less than 400,000 + 80,000 + 1000 + 30 + 6 is _____.

   c. 230,070 is _____ than 130,070.

2. Lucy plays an online math game. She scored 100,000 more points on Level 2 than on Level 3. If she scored 349,867 points on Level 2, what was her score on Level 3? Use pictures, words, or numbers to explain your thinking.

3. Complete the following equations:

    a.   10,000 + 40,060 = _____

    b.   21,195 − 10,000 = _____

    c.   999,000 + 1,000 = _____

    d.   129,231 − 100,000 = _____

    e.   122,000 = 22,000 + _____

    f.   38,018 = 39,018 − _____

4. Fill in the empty boxes to complete the patterns.

150,010		170,010		190,010	

    a.   Explain in pictures, numbers, and words how you found your answer.

	898,756	798,756			498,756

    b.   Explain in pictures, numbers, and words how you found your answer.

744,369	743,369		741,369		

    c.   Explain in pictures, numbers, and words how you found your answer.

	118,910			88,910	78,910

    d.   Explain in pictures, numbers, and words how you found your answer.

Name _____   Date _____

1. Fill in the empty boxes to complete the pattern.

468,235			471,235	472,235	

   a. Explain in pictures, numbers, and words how you found your answer.

2. Complete the following equations.

   a. $1,000 + 56,879 =$ _____

   b. $324,560 - 100,000 =$ _____

   c. $456,080 - 10,000 =$ _____

   d. $10,000 + 786,233 =$ _____

3. The population of Rochester, NY in the 1990 census was 219,782. The 2000 census found that the population decreased by about 10,000. About how many people lived in Rochester in 2000? Explain in pictures, numbers, and words how you found your answer.

COMMON CORE™

Lesson 6:   Find 1, 10, and 100 thousand more and less than a given number.
Date: 6/28/13

1.B.22

Name _____   Date _____

1. Label the place value chart. Use number disks to find the sum or difference. Write the answer in standard form on the line.

    a. 100,000 less than five hundred sixty thousand, three hundred thirteen is _____.

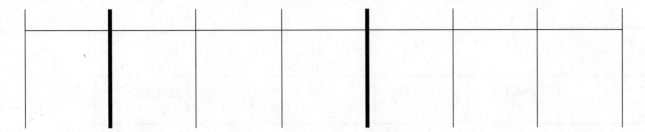

    b. Ten thousand more than 300,000 + 90,000 + 5000 + 40 is _____.

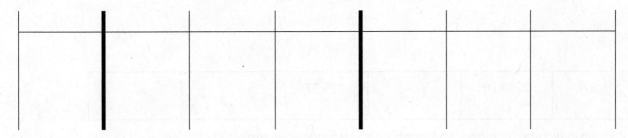

    c. 448,077 is _____ than 347,077.

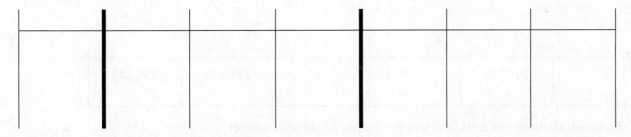

2. Complete the following equations:

    a. 100,000 + 76,960 = _____   b. 13,097 − 1,000 = _____

    c. 849,000 − 10,000 = _____   d. 442,210 + 10,000 = _____

    e. 172,090 = 171,090 + _____   f. 854,121 = 954,121 − _____

3. Fill in the empty boxes to complete the patterns.

| 145,555 | | 147,555 | | 149,555 | |

a. Explain in pictures, numbers, and words how you found your answer.

| | 764,321 | 774,321 | | | 804,321 |

b. Explain in pictures, numbers, and words how you found your answer.

| 125,876 | 225,876 | | 425,876 | | |

c. Explain in pictures, numbers, and words how you found your answer.

| | 254,445 | | | 224,445 | 214,445 |

d. Explain in pictures, numbers, and words how you found your answer.

4. In 2012, Charlie earned an annual salary of $54,098. At the beginning of 2013, Charlie's annual salary was raised by $10,000. How much money will Charlie earn in 2013? Use pictures, words, or numbers to explain your thinking.

COMMON CORE™

Lesson 6:   Find 1, 10, and 100 thousand more and less than a given number.
Date: 6/28/13

1.B.2

GRADE 4 • MODULE 1

Topic C
Rounding Multi-Digit Whole Numbers

4.NBT.3

Focus Standard:	4.NBT.3	Use place value understanding to round multi-digit whole numbers to any place.
Instructional Days:	4	
Coherence -Links from:	G3–M2	Place Value and Problem Solving with Units of Measure
-Links to:	G5–M1	Place Value and Decimal Fractions

In Topic C, students round to any place using the vertical number line and approximation. The vertical number line allows students to line up place values of the numbers they are comparing. In Grade 3, students rounded to the nearest 10 or 100 using place value understanding, and students extend this understanding rounding to the nearest thousand, ten thousand, and hundred thousand. Uniformity in the base ten system easily transfers understanding from the Grade 3 (**3.NBT.1**) to Grade 4 (**4.NBT.3**) standard. Rounding to the leftmost unit is easiest for students but Grade 4 students learn the advantages to rounding to any place value, which increases accuracy. Students move from dependency on the number line and learn to approximate the number to a particular unit. To round 34,108 to the nearest thousand, students find the nearest multiple, 34,000 or 35,000 by seeing if 34,108 is more than or less than half way between the multiples. The final concept will present complex and real world examples of rounding, such as instances where the number requires rounding down but the context requires rounding up.

A Teaching Sequence Towards Mastery of Rounding Multi-Digit Whole Numbers

Objective 1: Round multi-digit numbers to the thousands place using the vertical number line.
(Lesson 7)

Objective 2: Round multi-digit numbers to any place using the vertical number line.
(Lesson 8)

Objective 3: Use place value understanding to round multi-digit numbers to any place value.
(Lesson 9)

Objective 4: Use place value understanding to round multi-digit numbers to any place value using real world applications.
(Lesson 10)

Lesson 7

Objective: Round multi-digit numbers to the thousands place using the vertical number line.

Suggested Lesson Structure

- ■ Fluency Practice   (15 minutes)
- ■ Application Problem   (6 minutes)
- ■ Concept Development   (27 minutes)
- ■ Student Debrief   (12 minutes)
-   **Total Time**   **(60 minutes)**

Fluency Practice (15 minutes)

- Change Place Value **4.NBT.1**   (5 minutes)
- Number Patterns **4.NBT.1**   (5 minutes)
- Find the Midpoint **4.NBT.3**   (5 minutes)

Change Place Value (5 minutes)

Materials: (S) Personal white boards, place value chart to the millions

Note: This fluency will review Lesson 6's content.

T: (Project place value chart to the millions place. Write 3 hundred thousands, 5 ten thousands, 2 thousands, 1 hundred, 5 tens, and 4 ones.) On your personal boards, draw number disks and write the numbers beneath it.

S: (Students write.)

T: Show 100 more.

S: (Students write 1 more 100 disk, erase the number 1 in the hundreds place, and replace it with a 2 so that their boards read 352,254.)

Possible further sequence: 10,000 less, 100,000 more, 1 less, and 10 more.

T: (Write 300 + 80 + 5 =_____.) On your place value chart, write the number.

Possible further sequence: 7,000 + 300 + 80 + 5; 200,000 + 7,000 + 5 + 80; 300,000 + 6,000 + 30 + 2.

Number Patterns (5 minutes)

Materials: (S) Personal white boards

Note: This fluency will synthesize skip-counting fluency with Lesson 6's content and apply it in a context that lays a foundation for rounding multi-digit numbers to the thousands place.

> T: (Project 50,300; 60,300; 70,300; _____.) What is the place value of the digit that's changing?
> S: Ten thousand.
> T: Count with me saying the value of the digit I'm pointing to.
> S: (Point at the ten thousand digit as students count.) 50,000; 60,000; 70,000.
> T: On your personal boards, write what number would come after 70,300.
> S: Students write 80,300.

Repeat for the following possible sequence, using number disks if students are struggling:

92,010	82,010	72,010	_____
135,004	136,004	137,004	_____
832,743	832,643	832,543	_____
271,543	281,543	291,543	_____

Find the Midpoint (5 minutes)

Materials: (S) Personal white boards

Note: Practicing this skill in isolation will lay a foundation to conceptually understand rounding on a vertical number line.

Project a vertical line with endpoints 10 and 20.

> T: What's halfway between 10 and 20?
> S: 15.
> T: (Write 15 halfway between 10 and 20. Draw a second line with 1,000 and 2,000 as the endpoints.) How many hundreds are in 1,000?
> S: 10 hundreds.
> T: (Below 1,000 write 10 hundreds.) How many hundreds are in 2,000?
> S: 20 hundreds.

MP.2

> T: (Write 20 hundreds below 2,000.) What's halfway between 10 hundreds and 20 hundreds?
> S: 15 hundreds.
> T: (Write 1,500 halfway between 1,000 and 2,000. Below 1,500, write 15 hundreds.)
> T: On your personal boards, draw a number line with two endpoints and a midpoint.
> S: (Students draw number line with two endpoints and a midpoint.)
> T: Write 31,000 and 32,000 as endpoints.

number line

S: (Students write 31,000 and 32,000 as endpoints.)

T: How many hundreds are in 31,000?

S: 310 hundreds.

T: How many hundreds are in 32,000?

S: 320 hundreds.

T: Fill in the midpoint.

S: (Students write 31,500 as the midpoint.)

Repeat process and procedure to find the midpoint of 831,000 and 832,000; 63,000 and 64,000; 264,000 and 265,000; and 99,000 and 100,000.

Application Problems (6 minutes)

On Tuesday, according to her pedometer, Sarah took 42,619 steps. On Wednesday, Sarah took ten thousand more steps than she did on Tuesday. On Thursday, Sarah took one thousand fewer steps than she did on Wednesday. How many steps did Sarah take on Thursday?

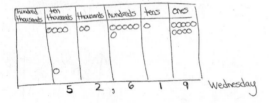 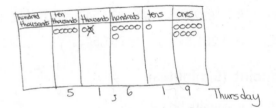

Note: This application problem builds on the concept of the previous lesson requiring students to find 1, 10, or 1,000 more or less than a given number.

Concept Development (27 minutes)

Materials: (S) Personal white boards

Problem 1

Use a vertical line to round a four-digit number to the nearest thousand.

T: (Draw a vertical number line with 2 endpoints.) How many thousands are in 4,100?

S: 4 thousands.

T: (Mark the lower endpoint with 4 thousands.) And 1 more thousand would be?

S: 5 thousands.

T: (Mark the upper endpoint with 5 thousands.) What's halfway between 4 thousands and 5 thousands?

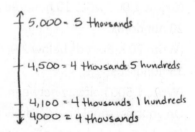

Lesson 7:   Round multi-digit numbers to the thousands place using the
               vertical number line.
Date: 6/28/13

© 2013 Common Core, Inc. All rights reserved. commoncore.org

1.C.4

S: 4,500.

T: (Mark 4,500 on the number line.) Where should I label 4,100? Tell me where to stop.

T: Is 4,100 nearer to 4 thousands or 5 thousands?

S: 4,100 is nearer to 4 thousands.

T: True. (Mark 4,700 on the number line.)

T: What about 4,700?

S: 4,700 is nearer to 5 thousands.

T: Therefore, we say 4,700 rounded to the nearest thousand is 5,000.

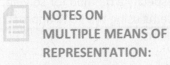

NOTES ON MULTIPLE MEANS OF REPRESENTATION:

For those students who have trouble conceptualizing *halfway*, demonstrate *halfway* using students as models. Two students represent the thousands. A third student represents halfway. A fourth student represents the number being rounded.
Discuss: Where do they belong? To whom are they nearer? To which number would they round?

Problem 2

Use a vertical line to round a five- and six-digit number to the nearest thousand.

T: Round 14,500 to the nearest thousand. How many thousands are there in 14,500?

S: 14 thousands.

T: What's 1 more thousand?

S: 15 thousands.

T: Designate the endpoints on your number line. What is halfway between 14,000 and 15,000?

S: 14,500.

T: Designate the halfway point on your number line. The halfway point is nearer to 15,000 so 14,500 rounded to the nearest thousand is 15,000.

T: With your partner, mark 14,990 on your number line and round it to the nearest thousand.

S: 14,990 is nearer to 15 thousands or 15,000.

T: Mark 14,345 on your number line. Talk with your partner about how to round it to the nearest thousand.

S: 14,345 is nearer to 14 thousands. → 14,345 is nearer to 14,000. → 14,345 rounded to the nearest thousand is 14,000.

T: Is 14,345 more than or less than the halfway point?

S: Less than.

T: We can look to see if 14,345 is closer to 14,000 or 15,000, and we can also look to see if it is greater than or less than the halfway point. If it is less than the halfway point, it is closer to 14,000.

Repeat using the numbers 215,711 and 214,569 rounding to the nearest thousand, naming how many thousands are in each number.

15,000 = 15 thousands

14,500 = 14 thousands 5 hundreds
14,345 = 14 thousands 3 hundreds

14,000 = 14 thousands

Lesson 7:   Round multi-digit numbers to the thousands place using the vertical number line.
Date: 6/28/13

1.C.5

Problem Set (10 minutes)

Students should do their personal best to complete the Problem Set within the allotted 10 minutes. For some classes, it may be appropriate to modify the assignment by specifying which problems they work on first. Some problems do not specify a method for solving. Students solve these problems using the RDW approach used for Application Problems.

Student Debrief (12 minutes)

Lesson Objective: Round multi-digit numbers to the thousands place using the vertical number line.

Invite students to review their solutions for the Problem Set and the totality of the lesson experience. They should check work by comparing answers with a partner before going over answers as a class. Look for misconceptions or misunderstandings that can be addressed in the Debrief. Guide students in a conversation to debrief the Problem Set. You may choose to use any combination of the questions below to lead the discussion.

- Look at Problem 1 in the Problem Set. Compare how you rounded 6,700 and 16,401. Explain how your rounding to the nearest thousand differed even though both numbers have a 6 in the thousands place.

- What was your strategy for solving Problem 4? How did the number line support your thinking?

- How are *fives* related to rounding?

- How does the number line help you round numbers? Is there another way you prefer? Why?

- What is the purpose of rounding?

- When might we use rounding or estimation?

Exit Ticket (3 minutes)

After the Student Debrief, instruct students to complete the Exit Ticket. A review of their work will help you assess the students' understanding of the concepts that were presented in the lesson today and plan more effectively for future lessons. You may read the questions aloud to the students.

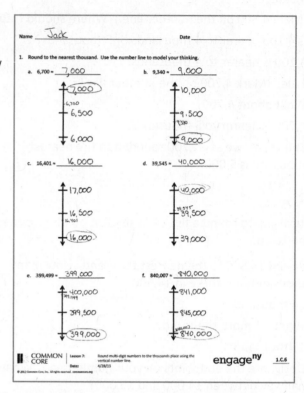

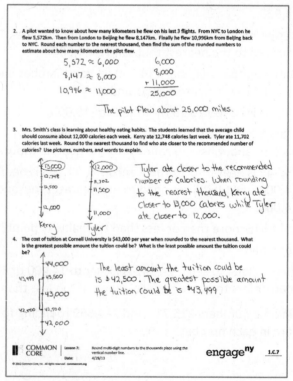

Lesson 7:   Round multi-digit numbers to the thousands place using the
Date: vertical number line.
               6/28/13

1.C.6

Name _____   Date _____

1. Round to the nearest thousand. Use the number line to model your thinking.

   a. 6,700 ≈ _____

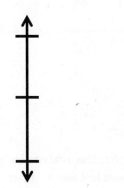

   b. 9,340 ≈ _____

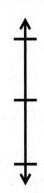

   c. 16,401 ≈ _____

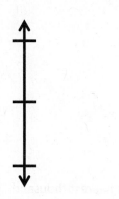

   d. 39,545 ≈ _____

   e. 399,499 ≈ _____

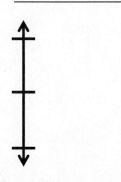

   f. 840,007 ≈ _____

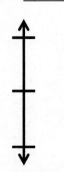

COMMON CORE™

Lesson 7: Round multi-digit numbers to the thousands place using the vertical number line.

Date: 6/28/13

1.C.7

2. A pilot wanted to know about how many kilometers he flew on his last 3 flights. From NYC to London he flew 5,572 km. Then, from London to Beijing he flew 8,147 km. Finally, he flew 10,996 km from Beijing back to NYC. Round each number to the nearest thousand, then find the sum of the rounded numbers to estimate about how many kilometers the pilot flew.

3. Mrs. Smith's class is learning about healthy eating habits. The students learned that the average child should consume about 12,000 calories each week. Kerry consumed 12,748 calories last week. Tyler consumed 11,702 calories last week. Round to the nearest thousand to find who consumed closer to the recommended number of calories? Use pictures, numbers, and words to explain.

4. The cost of tuition at Cornell University is $43,000 per year when rounded to the nearest thousand. What is the greatest possible amount the tuition could be? What is the least possible amount the tuition could be?

Name _____   Date _____

1. Round to the nearest thousand. Use the number line to model your thinking.

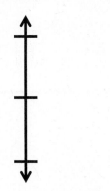      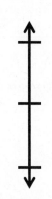

   a. 7,621 ≈ _____   b. 12,502 ≈ _____   c. 324,087 ≈ _____

2. It takes 39,090 gallons of water to manufacture a new car. Sammy thinks that rounds up to about 40,000 gallons. Susie thinks it is about 39,000 gallons. Who rounded to the nearest thousand, Sammy or Susie? Use pictures numbers and words to explain.

COMMON CORE™   Lesson 7:   Round multi-digit numbers to the thousands place using the   **1.C.9**
                              vertical number line.
                    Date: 6/28/13

Name _____   Date _____

1. Round to the nearest thousand. Use the number line to model your thinking.

a.   5,900 ≈ _____

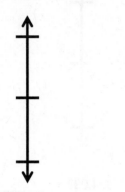

b.   4,180 ≈ _____

c.   32,879 ≈ _____

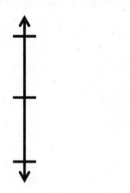

d.   78,600 ≈ _____

e.   251,031 ≈ _____

f.   699,900 ≈ _____

COMMON CORE™ | Lesson 7:   Round multi-digit numbers to the thousands place using the vertical number line.
Date: 6/28/13

1.C.10

2. Steven and his friend were putting together a 5,000 piece puzzle. In one day, they put together 981 of the pieces. About how many pieces did they put together? Round to the nearest thousand. Use what you know about place value to explain your answer.

3. Louise's family went on vacation to Disney World. Their vacation cost $5,990. Sophia's family went on vacation to Niagara Falls. Their vacation cost $4,720. Both families budgeted about $5,000 for their vacation. Whose family stayed closer to the budget? Round to the nearest thousand. Use what you know about place value to explain your answer.

4. Marsha's brother wanted help with the first question on his homework. The question asked the students to round 128,902 to the nearest thousand and then to explain the answer. Marsha's brother thought that the answer was 128,000. Was his answer correct? How do you know? Use pictures, numbers, and words to explain what you know about place value.

Lesson 7:   Round multi-digit numbers to the thousands place using the vertical number line.

Date: 6/28/13

1.C.11

Lesson 8

Objectives: Round multi-digit numbers to any place using the vertical number line.

Suggested Lesson Structure

■ Fluency Practice   (12 minutes)
■ Application Problem   (6 minutes)
■ Concept Development   (32 minutes)
■ Student Debrief   (10 minutes)
   Total Time   **(60 minutes)**

Fluency Practice (12 minutes)

▪ Find the Halfway Point **4.NBT.3**   (9 minutes)
▪ Rename the Units **4.NBT.2**   (3 minutes)

Sprint: Find the Midpoint (9 minutes)

Materials: (S) Find the Halfway Point Sprint

Note: Practicing this skill in isolation will lay a foundation to conceptually understand rounding on a vertical number line.

Rename the Units (3 minutes)

Materials: (S) Personal white boards

Note: This fluency applies students' place value skills in a new context that will help them better access the lesson's content.

   T: (Write 357,468.) Say the number.
   S: 357,468.
   T: (Write 357,468 = _____ thousands 468 ones.) On your personal white boards, fill in the number sentence.
   S: (Students write 357,468 = 357 thousands 468 ones.)

Repeat process for 357,468 = _____ ten thousands 7468 ones; 357,468 = _____ hundreds 6 tens 8 ones; 357,468 = _____ tens 8 ones.

Lesson 8:   Round multi-digit numbers to any place value using the vertical
             number line.
Date: 6/28/13

1.C.12

Application Problem (6 minutes)

Jose's parents bought a used car, a new motorcycle, and a used snowmobile. The car cost $8,999. The motorcycle cost $9,690. The snowmobile cost $4,419. About how much money did they spend on the three items?

Car $8,999 ≈ $9,000
Motorcycle $9,690 ≈ $10,000
Snowmobile $4,419 ≈ $4,000
9 thousands + 10 thousands + 4 thousands = 23 thousands
Jose's parents spent about $23,000.

Note: Application problem builds on the content of previous lessons. Students are required to round and then to add base thousand units.

Concept Development (32 minutes)

Materials: (S) Personal white boards

Problem 1

Use a vertical number line to round five- and six-digit numbers to the nearest ten thousand.

(Display a number line with endpoints 70,000 and 80,000.)

T: (Draw a number line to round 72,744 to the nearest ten thousand.) How many ten thousands are in 72,744?

80,000 = 8 ten thousands
75,000 = 7 ten thousands 5 thousands
72,744 = 7 ten thousands 2 thousands
70,000 = 7 ten thousands

S: 7 ten thousands.

T: (Mark the lower endpoint with 7 ten thousands.) And 1 more ten thousand would be?

S: 8 ten thousands.

T: (Mark the upper endpoint with 8 ten thousands.) What's halfway between 7 ten thousands and 8 ten thousands?

S: 7 ten thousands 5 thousands. → 75,000.

T: (Mark 75,000 on the number line.) Where should I label 72,744? Tell me where to stop. (Move your marker up the line.)

T: Is 72,744 nearer to 70,000 or 80,000?

S: 72,744 is nearer to 70,000.

T: We can say 72,755 rounded to the nearest ten thousand is 70,000.

Repeat with 337,601 rounded to the nearest ten thousand.

An effective scaffold when working in the thousands period is to first work with an analogous number in the ones period. For example:

T: Let's round 72 to the nearest ten.

T: How many tens are in 72?

S: 7 tens.

T: What is 1 more ten?

S: 8 tens.

T: 7 tens and 8 tens are the endpoints of my number line.

T: What is the value of the halfway point?

S: 7 tens 5 ones. → Seventy-five.

T: Tell me where to stop on my number line (Start at 70 and move up.)

S: Stop!

T: Is 72 less than halfway or more than halfway to 8 tens or 80?

S: Less than halfway.

T: We say 72 rounded to the nearest ten is 70.

T: We use the exact same process when rounding 72 thousand to the nearest ten thousand.

Lesson 8:   Round multi-digit numbers to any place value using the vertical number line.
Date: 6/28/13

1.C.13

Problem 2

Use a vertical number line to round a six-digit number to the nearest hundred thousand.

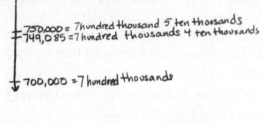

T: (Draw a number line to round 749,085 to the nearest hundred thousand.) How many hundred thousands are in 749,085?

S: 7 hundred thousands.

T: What's 1 more hundred thousand?

S: 8 hundred thousand.

T: Label your endpoints on the number line. What is halfway between 7 hundred thousand and 8 hundred thousand?

S: 7 hundred thousand 5 ten thousands. → 750,000.

T: Designate the midpoint on the number line. With your partner, mark 749,085 on the number line and round it to the nearest hundred thousand.

S: 749,085 is nearer to 7 hundred thousands. → 749,085 is nearest to 700,000. → 749,085 rounded to the nearest hundred thousand is 700,000.

Repeat with 908,899 rounded to the nearest hundred thousand.

Problem 3

Estimating with addition and subtraction.

(Write 505,341 + 193,841.)

T: Without finding the actual answer, I can estimate the answer by rounding each addend to the nearest hundred thousand and then add the rounded numbers.

T: Use a number line to round both numbers to the nearest hundred thousand.

S: Round 505,341 to 500,000. Round 193,841 to 200,000.

T: Now add 500,000 + 200,000.

S: 700,000.

T: So, what's a good estimate of the sum of 505,341 and 193,841?

S: 700,000.

T: (Write 35,555 – 26,555.) How can we use rounding to estimate the answer?

S: Let's round each number before we subtract.

T: Good idea. Discuss with your partner how you will round to estimate the difference.

S: I can round each number to the nearest ten thousand. That way I'll have mostly zeros in my numbers. 40,000 minus 30,000 is 10,000. → 35,555 minus 26,555 is like 35 minus 26 which is 9. 35,000 minus 26,000 is 9,000. → It's more accurate to round up. 36,000 minus 27,000 is 9,000. Hey, it's the same answer!

MP.2

> **NOTES ON MULTIPLE MEANS OF ENGAGEMENT:**
>
> For students working below grade level, make the lesson relevant to their lives. Discuss everyday instances of estimation. Elicit examples of our frequent use of a general idea of a sum or difference—rather than the exact answer. Ask, "When is it appropriate to estimate? When do we need an exact answer?"

COMMON CORE™

Lesson 8:

Date:

Round multi-digit numbers to any place value using the vertical number line.

6/28/13

1.C.14

T: What did you discover?

S: It's easier to find an estimate rounded to the largest unit. → We found the same estimate even though he rounded up and I rounded down. → We got two different estimates!

T: Which estimate do you suppose is closer to the actual difference?

S: I think 9,000 is closer because we changed fewer numbers when we rounded.

T: How might we find an estimate even closer to the actual difference?

S: We could round to the nearest hundred or ten.

Problem Set (10 minutes)

Students should do their personal best to complete the Problem Set within the allotted 10 minutes. For some classes, it may be appropriate to modify the assignment by specifying which problems they work on first. Some problems do not specify a method for solving. Students solve these problems using the RDW approach used for Application Problems.

Student Debrief (10 minutes)

Lesson Objective: Round multi-digit numbers to any place value using the vertical number line.

Invite students to review their solutions for the Problem Set and the totality of the lesson experience. They should check work by comparing answers with a partner before going over answers as a class. Look for misconceptions or misunderstandings that can be addressed in the Debrief. Guide students in a conversation to debrief the Problem Set. You may choose to use any combination of the questions below to lead the discussion.

- Compare Problems 1(b) and 1(c). How did you determine your endpoints for each number line?

- Retell to your partner your steps for rounding a number. Which step is most difficult for you? Why?

- How did Problem 1(c) help you to find the missing number possibilities in Problem 4?

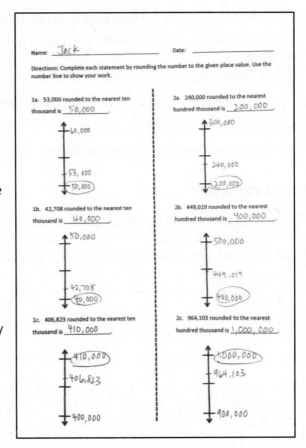

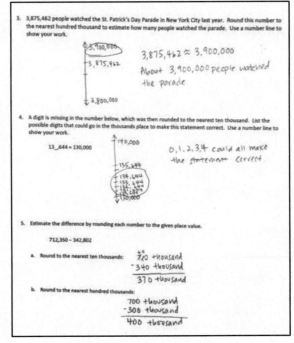

Lesson 8:   Round multi-digit numbers to any place value using the vertical number line.
Date: 6/28/13

1.C.15

- Look at Problem 5. How did your estimates compare? What did you notice as you solved?
- What are the benefits and drawbacks of rounding the same number to different units (as you did in Problem 5)?
- In what real life situation might you make an estimate like Problem 5?

Write and complete one of the following statements in your math journal:

- The purpose of rounding addends is _____.
- Rounding to the nearest _____ is best when _____.

Exit Ticket (3 minutes)

After the Student Debrief, instruct students to complete the Exit Ticket. A review of their work will help you assess the students' understanding of the concepts that were presented in the lesson today and plan more effectively for future lessons. You may read the questions aloud to the students.

Lesson 8: Round multi-digit numbers to any place value using the vertical number line.

Date: 6/28/13

1.C.16

A   # Correct _____

Find the halfway point.

1	0	10	23	6000	7000
2	0	100	24	600	700
3	0	1000	25	60	70
4	10	20	26	260	270
5	100	200	27	9260	9270
6	1000	2000	28	80	90
7	30	40	29	90	100
8	300	400	30	990	1000
9	400	500	31	9990	10,000
10	20	30	32	440	450
11	30	40	33	8300	8400
12	40	50	34	680	690
13	50	60	35	9400	9500
14	500	600	36	3900	4000
15	5000	6000	37	2450	2460
16	200	300	38	7080	7090
17	300	400	39	3200	3210
18	700	800	40	8630	8640
19	5700	5800	41	8190	8200
20	70	80	42	2510	2520
21	670	680	43	4890	4900
22	6700	6800	44	6660	6670

© Bill Davidson

Lesson 8:   Round multi-digit numbers to any place value using the vertical number line.

Date: 6/28/13

1.C.17

B

Find the halfway point.   Improvement _____   # Correct _____

1	10	20	23	7000	8000
2	100	200	24	700	800
3	1000	2000	25	70	80
4	20	30	26	270	280
5	200	300	27	9270	9280
6	2000	3000	28	80	90
7	40	50	29	90	100
8	400	500	30	990	1000
9	500	600	31	9990	10,000
10	30	40	32	450	460
11	40	50	33	8400	8500
12	50	60	34	580	590
13	60	70	35	9500	9600
14	600	700	36	2900	3000
15	6000	7000	37	3450	3460
16	300	400	38	6080	6090
17	400	500	39	4200	4210
18	800	900	40	7630	7640
19	5800	5900	41	7190	7200
20	80	90	42	3510	3520
21	680	690	43	5890	5900
22	6800	6900	44	7770	7780

© Bill Davidson

COMMON CORE™

Lesson 8:   Round multi-digit numbers to any place value using the vertical number line.

Date: 6/28/13

1.C.18

Name _____   Date _____

Directions: Complete each statement by rounding the number to the given place value. Use the number line to show your work.

1a. 53,000 rounded to the nearest ten thousand is _____.

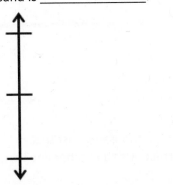

2a. 240,000 rounded to the nearest hundred thousand is _____.

1b. 42,708 rounded to the nearest ten thousand is _____.

2b. 449,019 rounded to the nearest hundred thousand is _____.

1c. 406,823 rounded to the nearest ten thousand is _____.

2c. 964,103 rounded to the nearest hundred thousand is _____.

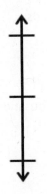

COMMON CORE™   Lesson 8:   Round multi-digit numbers to any place value using the vertical number line.

Date: 6/28/13

1.C.19

© 2013 Common Core, Inc. All rights reserved. commoncore.org

3. 3,875,462 people watched the St. Patrick's Day Parade in New York City last year. Round this number to the nearest hundred thousand to estimate how many people watched the parade. Use a number line to show your work.

4. A digit is missing in the number below, which was then rounded to the nearest ten thousand. List the possible digits that could go in the thousands place to make this statement correct. Use a number line to show your work.

    13_,644 ≈ 130,000

5. Estimate the difference by rounding each number to the given place value.

    712,350 – 342,802

    a. Round to the nearest ten thousands.

    b. Round to the nearest hundred thousands.

COMMON CORE™ Lesson 8: Round multi-digit numbers to any place value using the vertical number line.
Date: 6/28/13

1.C.20

Name _____   Date _____

1. Round to the nearest ten thousand. Use the number line to model your thinking.

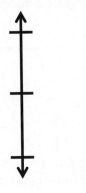   

    a. 35,124 ≈ _____   b. 981,657 ≈ _____

2. Round to the nearest hundred thousand. Use the number line to model your thinking.

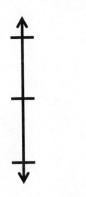   

    a. 89,678 ≈ _____   b. 999,765 ≈ _____

3. Estimate the sum by rounding each number to the nearest hundred thousand.

    257,098 + 548,765 ≈ _____

Name _____   Date _____

Directions: Complete each statement by rounding the number to the given place value. Use the number line to show your work.

1a. 67,000 rounded to the nearest ten thousand
is _____.

1b. 51,988 rounded to the nearest ten thousand
is _____.

1c. 105,159 rounded to the nearest ten thousand
is _____.

2a. 867,000 rounded to the nearest hundred
thousand is _____.

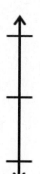

2b. 767,074 rounded to the nearest hundred
thousand is _____.

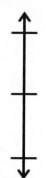

2c. 629,999 rounded to the nearest hundred
thousand is _____.

3. 491,852 people went to the water park in the month of July. Round this number to the nearest hundred thousand to estimate how many people went to the park. Use a number line to show your work.

4. A digit is missing in the number below, which was then rounded to the nearest hundred thousand. List the possible digits that could go in the ten thousands place to make this statement correct. Use a number line to show your work.

$$1\_9,644 \approx 100,000$$

5. Estimate the sum by rounding each number to the given place value.

$$164,215 + 216,088$$

a. Round to the nearest ten thousands.

b. Round to the nearest hundred thousands.

COMMON CORE™

Lesson 8:   Round multi-digit numbers to any place value using the vertical number line.

Date: 6/28/13

1.C.23

© 2013 Common Core, Inc. All rights reserved. commoncore.org

Lesson 9

Objective: Use place value understanding to round multi-digit numbers to any place value.

Suggested Lesson Structure

■ Fluency Practice　　　　(12 minutes)
■ Application Problem　　　(8 minutes)
■ Concept Development　　(30 minutes)
■ Student Debrief　　　　(10 minutes)
　Total Time　　　　　**(60 minutes)**

Fluency Practice (12 minutes)

▪ Multiply by Ten **4.NBT.1**　　　　(5 minutes)
▪ Round to Different Place Values **4.NBT.3**　　(7 minutes)

Multiply by Ten (5 minutes)

Materials: (S) Personal white boards

Note: This fluency will deepen the students' foundation of multiplying by ten.

　T:　(Write 10 x 10 =_____.) Say the multiplication sentence.
　S:　10 x 10 = 100.
　T:　(Write 10 x _____ ten = 100.) On your boards, fill in the blank.

Students write 10 x 1 ten = 100.

T:　　(Write _____ ten x _____ ten = 100.) On your boards, fill in the blank.

Students write 1 ten x 1 ten = 100.

T:　　(Write _____ ten x _____ ten = _____hundred.) On your personal white boards, fill in the blank.

Students write 1 ten x 1 ten = 1 hundred.

Repeat process for possible sequence: 1 ten x 20 =_____, 1 ten x 40 = _____ hundreds, 1 ten x _____= 700, 4 tens x 1 ten = _____ hundreds.

Note: The use of the digit or a unit is intentional. It builds understanding of multiplying by different units (6 ones times 1 ten equals 6 tens, so 6 tens times 1 ten equals 6 hundreds, not 6 tens).

COMMON CORE™　| Lesson 9:　| Use place value understanding to round multi-digit numbers
　　　　　　　　　|　　　　　| to any place value.　　　　　　　　　　　　　　　　　　　　　　　1.C.24
　　　　　　　　　| Date:　　| 6/28/13

Round to Different Place Values (7 minutes)

Materials: (S) Personal white boards

Note: This fluency will review Lesson 8's objective and lay a foundation for today's lesson.

- T: (Write 63,941.) Say the number.
- S: 63,941.
- T: Between what 2 ten thousands is 63,941?
- S: 60 thousand and 70 thousand.
- T: On your boards, write a vertical number line with 60,000 and 70,000 as endpoints.

Students write a vertical number line with 60,000 and 70,000 as the endpoints.

- T: What's halfway between 60,000 and 70,000?
- S: 65,000.
- T: Label 65,000 as the midpoint on your number line. Label 63,941 on your number line.

Students write 63,941 below 65,000 on their number lines.

- T: (Write 63,941 ≈ _____.) On your boards, fill in the blank, rounding 63,941 to the nearest ten thousand.

Students write 63,941 ≈ 60,000.

Repeat process for 63,941 rounded to the nearest thousand, 47,261 rounded to the nearest ten thousand, 47,261 rounded to the nearest thousand, 618,409 rounded to the nearest hundred thousand, 618,409 rounded to the nearest ten thousand, 618,904 rounded to the nearest thousand.

Application Problem (8 minutes)

34,123 people attended a basketball game. 28,310 people attended a football game. About how many more people attended the basketball game than the football game? Round to the nearest ten thousands to find the answer. Does your answer make sense? What might be a better way to compare attendance?

Note: The application problem builds on the concept learned in the previous lesson **(4.NBT.3)** and on **3.NBT.2**. Students are required to round and then to subtract using base thousand units. Students have not practiced an algorithm for subtracting with five digits. Due to the rounded numbers, the teacher may show subtraction using unit names as an alternative method (34 thousand − 28 thousand, instead of 34,000 − 28,000).

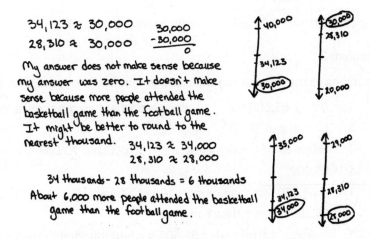

Lesson 9:	Use place value understanding to round multi-digit numbers to any place value.
Date:	6/28/13

1.C.25

© 2013 Common Core, Inc. All rights reserved. **commoncore.org**

Concept Development (30 minutes)

Materials: (S) Personal white boards

Problem 1

Rounding to the nearest thousand without using a number line.

T: (Write 4,333 ≈ _____.) Between what two thousands is 4,333?

S: 4 thousand and 5 thousand.

T: What is halfway between 4,000 and 5,000?

S: 4,500.

T: Is 4,333 less than or more than halfway?

S: Less than.

T: So 4,333 is nearer to 4,000.

T: (Write 18,753 ≈_____.) Tell your partner between what two thousands 18,753 is located.

S: 18 thousands and 19 thousands.

T: What is halfway between 18 thousand and 19 thousand?

S: 18,500.

T: Round 18,753 to the nearest thousand. Tell your partner if 18,753 is more than or less than halfway.

S: 18,753 is more than halfway. 18,753 is nearer to 19,000. → 18,753 rounded to the nearest thousand is 19,000.

4,333 ≈ ?
_____

> **NOTES ON MULTIPLE MEANS OF REPRESENTATION:**
>
> Students who are having difficulty visualizing 4,333 as having 4 thousands 3 hundreds could benefit from writing the number on their place value chart. In doing so, they will be able to see that 4,333 has 43 hundreds. This same strategy could also be used for other numbers.

Repeat with 346,560 rounded to the nearest thousand.

Problem 2

Rounding to the nearest ten thousand or hundred thousand without using a vertical line.

T: (Write 65,600 ≈ _____.) Between what two ten thousands is 65,600?

S: 60,000 and 70,000.

T: Name what is halfway between 60,000 and 70,000.

S: 65,000.

T: Is 65,600 less than or more than halfway.

S: 65,600 is more than halfway.

T: Tell your partner what 65,600 is when rounded to the nearest ten thousand.

S: 65,600 rounded to the nearest ten thousand is 70,000.

Lesson 9: Use place value understanding to round multi-digit numbers to any place value.
Date: 6/28/13

1.C.26

Repeat with the number 548,253 rounded to the nearest ten thousand.

T: (Write 676,000 ≈ ____.) Round 676,000 to the nearest hundred thousand. First tell your partner what your endpoints will be.

S: 600,000 and 700,000.

T: Determine the halfway point.

S: 650,000.

T: Is 676,000 more than or less than the halfway point?

S: More than.

T: Tell your partner what 676,000 is when rounded to the nearest hundred thousand.

S: 676,000 rounded to the nearest hundred thousand is 700,000.

T: (Write 203,301 ≈ ____.) Work with your partner to round 203,301 to the nearest hundred thousand.

T: Explain to your partner how we use the midpoint to round without a number line.

S: We can't look at a number line, so we have to use mental math to find our endpoints and halfway point. → If we know the midpoint, we can see if the number is greater than or less than the midpoint. → When rounding, the midpoint determines if our number is closer to the unit we are rounding to or if we have to round up to the next unit.

Problem 3

Rounding to any value without using a number line.

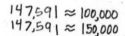

T: (Write 147,591 ≈ ____.) Whisper read this number to your partner in standard form. Now, round 147,591 to the nearest hundred thousand.

S: 100,000.

T: Excellent. (Write 147,591 ≈ 100,000. Point.) 100,000 has no ones in the ones place, no tens in the tens place, no hundreds in the hundreds place, no thousands in the thousands place, and no ten thousands in the ten thousands place. I could add, subtract, multiply, or divide with this rounded number much easier than with 147,591. True? But, what if I wanted a more accurate estimate? Give me a number closer to 147,591 that has (point) a zero in the ones, tens, hundreds, and thousands.

S: 150,000.

T: Why not 140,000?

S: 147,591 is closer to 150,000 because it is greater than the halfway point 145,000.

T: Great. 147,591 rounded to the nearest ten thousand is 150,000. Now let's round 147,591 to the nearest thousand.

S: 148,000.

NOTES ON MULTIPLE MEANS OF ENGAGEMENT:

Challenge students above grade level to look at the many ways that they rounded the number 147,591 to different place values. Have them discuss with a partner what they notice about the rounded numbers. Students should notice that when rounding to the hundred thousands that the answer is 100,000, but when rounding to all of the other places that the answers are closer to 150,000. Have them discuss what this can teach us about rounding.

Lesson 9:   Use place value understanding to round multi-digit numbers
             to any place value.
Date: 6/28/13

1.C.27

MP.3

T: Work with your partner to round 147,591 to the nearest hundred and then the nearest ten.

S: 147,591 rounded to the nearest hundred is 147,600. 147,591 rounded to the nearest ten is 147,590.

T: Compare estimates of 147,591 after rounding to different units. What do you notice? When might it be better to round to a larger unit? When might it be better to round to a smaller unit?

S: (Students discuss.)

Problem Set (10 minutes)

Students should do their personal best to complete the Problem Set within the allotted 10 minutes. For some classes, it may be appropriate to modify the assignment by specifying which problems they work on first. Some problems do not specify a method for solving. Students solve these problems using the RDW approach used for Application Problems.

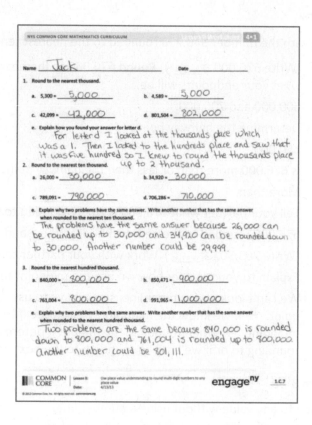

Student Debrief (10 minutes)

Lesson Objective: Use place value understanding to round multi-digit numbers to any place value.

Invite students to review their solutions for the Problem Set and the totality of the lesson experience. They should check work by comparing answers with a partner before going over answers as a class. Look for misconceptions or misunderstandings that can be addressed in the Debrief. Guide students in a conversation to debrief the Problem Set. You may choose to use any combination of the questions below to lead the discussion.

- Explain the reasoning behind your answer for Problems 2(e) and 3(e).

- In Problem 2(e), you and your partner probably wrote different numbers that rounded to 30,000. Explain why your numbers were different. What is the smallest possible number that could round to 30,000 when rounded to the nearest ten thousand? What is the largest possible number

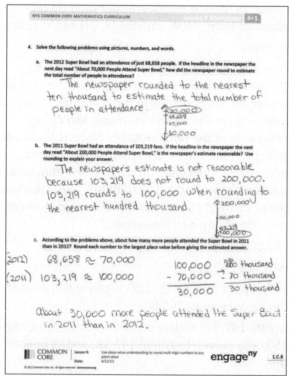

Lesson 9:   Use place value understanding to round multi-digit numbers to any place value.
Date: 6/28/13

1.C.28

that could round to 30,000 when rounded to the nearest ten thousand? Explain your reasoning. (Use Problem 3(e) for further discussion.)

- Was there any difficulty in solving Problem 3(d)? Explain your strategy when solving this problem.
- In Problem 4(b), the newspaper rounded to the nearest hundred thousand inappropriately. What unit should the newspaper rounded to and why?
- How is rounding without a number line easier? How is it more challenging?
- How does knowing how to round mentally assist you in everyday life?
- What strategy do you use when observing a number to be rounded?

Exit Ticket (3 minutes)

After the Student Debrief, instruct students to complete the Exit Ticket. A review of their work will help you assess the students' understanding of the concepts that were presented in the lesson today and plan more effectively for future lessons. You may read the questions aloud to the students.

| Lesson 9: | Use place value understanding to round multi-digit numbers to any place value. | 1.C.29 |
| Date: | 6/28/13 | |

© 2013 Common Core, Inc. All rights reserved. commoncore.org

Name _____   Date _____

1. Round to the nearest thousand.

    a. 5,300 ≈ _____   b. 4,589 ≈ _____

    c. 42,099 ≈ _____   d. 801,504 ≈ _____

    e. Explain how you found your answer for Part (d).

2. Round to the nearest ten thousand.

    a. 26,000 ≈ _____   b. 34,920 ≈ _____

    c. 789,091 ≈ _____   d. 706,286 ≈ _____

    e. Explain why two problems have the same answer. Write another number that has the same answer
        when rounded to the nearest ten thousand.

3. Round to the nearest hundred thousand.

    a. 840,000 ≈ _____   b. 850,471 ≈ _____

    c. 761,004 ≈ _____   d. 991,965 ≈ _____

    e. Explain why two problems have the same answer. Write another number that has the same answer
        when rounded to the nearest hundred thousand.

COMMON CORE™   Lesson 9:   Use place value understanding to round multi-digit numbers
to any place value.
Date: 6/28/13   1.C.30

4. Solve the following problems using pictures, numbers, and words.

   a. The 2012 Super Bowl had an attendance of just 68,658 people. If the headline in the newspaper the next day read "About 70,000 People Attend Super Bowl," how did the newspaper round to estimate the total number of people in attendance?

   b. The 2011 Super Bowl had an attendance of 103,219 fans. If the headline in the newspaper the next day read "About 200,000 People Attend Super Bowl," is the newspaper's estimate reasonable? Use rounding to explain your answer.

   c. According to the problems above, about how many more people attended the Super Bowl in 2011 than in 2012? Round each number to the largest place value before giving the estimated answer.

COMMON CORE™ | Lesson 9: | Use place value understanding to round multi-digit numbers to any place value. | 1.C.31
Date: | 6/28/13

© 2013 Common Core, Inc. All rights reserved. commoncore.org

Name _____ Date _____

1. Round 765,903 to the given place value:

    Thousand _____

    Ten thousand _____

    Hundred thousand _____

2. There are 16,850 Star coffee shops around the world. Round the number of shops to the nearest thousand and ten thousand. Which answer is more accurate? Explain your thinking using pictures, numbers and words.

COMMON CORE™

Lesson 9:   Use place value understanding to round multi-digit numbers to any place value.

Date: 6/28/13

1.C.32

Name _____   Date _____

1. Round to the nearest thousand.

    a. 6,842 ≈ _____   b. 2,722 ≈ _____

    c. 16,051 ≈ _____   d. 706,421 ≈ _____

    e. Explain how you found your answer for Part (d).

2. Round to the nearest ten thousand.

    a. 88,999 ≈ _____   b. 85,001 ≈ _____

    c. 789,091 ≈ _____   d. 905,154 ≈ _____

    e. Explain why two problems have the same answer. Write another number that has the same answer
        when rounded to the nearest ten thousand.

3. Round to the nearest hundred thousand.

    a. 89,659 ≈ _____   b. 751,447 ≈ _____

    c. 617,889 ≈ _____   d. 817,245 ≈ _____

    e. Explain why two problems have the same answer. Write another number that has the same answer
        when rounded to the nearest hundred thousand.

COMMON CORE™ | Lesson 9: Use place value understanding to round multi-digit numbers   1.C.33
                            to any place value.
                   Date: 6/28/13

4. Solve the following problems using pictures, numbers, and words.

   a. At President Obama's inauguration in 2013, the newspaper headlines stated there were about 800,000 people in attendance. If the newspaper rounded to the nearest hundred thousand, what is the largest number and smallest number of people that could have been there?

   b. At President Bush's inauguration in 2005, the newspaper headlines stated there were about 400,000 people in attendance. If the newspaper rounded to the nearest ten thousand, what is the largest number and smallest number of people that could have been there?

   c. At President Lincoln's inauguration in 1861, the newspaper headlines stated there were about 30,000 people in attendance. If the newspaper rounded to the nearest thousand, what is the largest number and smallest number of people that could have been there?

Lesson 10

Objective: Use place value understanding to round multi-digit numbers to any place value using real world applications.

Suggested Lesson Structure

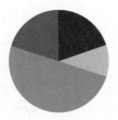

- ■ Fluency Practice   (12 minutes)
- ▨ Application Problem   (6 minutes)
- ▨ Concept Development   (30 minutes)
- ■ Student Debrief   (12 minutes)
  - **Total Time**   **(60 minutes)**

Fluency Practice (12 minutes)

- Round to the Nearest 10,000 **4.NBT.3**   (9 minutes)
- Multiply by Ten **4.NBT.1**   (3 minutes)

Sprint: Round to the Nearest 10,000 (9 minutes)

Materials: (S) Round to the Nearest 10,000 Sprint

Note: This fluency will review Lesson 9's content and work towards automatizing rounding skills.

Multiply by Ten (3 minutes)

Materials: (S) Personal white boards

Note: This fluency will deepen student understanding of base ten units.

   T: (Write 10 x 10 =____.) Say the multiplication sentence.

   S: 10 x 10 = 100.

   T: (Write ____ten x 10 = 100.) On your boards, fill in the blank.

Students write 1 ten x 10 = 100.

   T: (Write ____ten x ____ten = 100.) On your boards, fill in the blanks.

Students write 1 ten x 1 ten = 100.

   T: (Write ____ten x ____ten = ____hundred.) On your boards, fill in the blanks.

Students write 1 ten x 1 ten = 1 hundred.

Lesson 10:   Use place value understanding to round multi-digit numbers to
           any place value using real world applications.
Date: 6/28/13

1.C.35

Repeat using the following sequence: 1 ten x 50 =____, 1 ten x 80 = ____hundreds, 1 ten x ____= 600.
3 tens x 1 ten = ____hundreds.

Note: Watch for students who say 3 tens x 4 tens is 12 tens rather than 12 hundreds.

Application Problem (6 minutes)

The post office sold 204,789 stamps last week and 93,061 stamps this week. About how many more stamps did the post office sell last week than this week? Explain how you got your answer.

Note: This application problem builds on the concept of the previous lesson (rounding multi-digit numbers to any place value) and creates a bridge to this lesson's concept (rounding using real world applications).

$204,789 \approx 200,000$

$93,061 \approx 90,000$

200 thousands - 90 thousands = 110 thousands
The post office sold about 110,000 more stamps last week than this week. I got my answer by rounding to the nearest ten thousand and then subtracting.

Concept Development (30 minutes)

Materials: (S) Personal white boards

Introduction

T: Write 935,292≈____. Read it to your partner and round to the nearest hundred thousand.

S: 900,000.

T: It is 900,000 when we round to the largest unit. What's the next largest unit we might round to?

S: Ten thousands.

T: Round to the ten thousands. Then round to the thousands.

S: 940,000. 935,000.

T: What changes about the numbers when rounding to smaller and smaller units? Discuss with your partner.

S: When you round to the largest unit, every other place will have a zero. → Rounding to the largest unit gives you the easiest number to add, subtract, multiply, or divide. → As you round to smaller units, there are not as many zeros in the number. → Rounding to smaller units gives an estimate that is closer to the actual value of the number.

$935,292 \approx 900,000$

$935,292 \approx 940,000$

$935,292 \approx 935,000$

Lesson 10:   Use place value understanding to round multi-digit numbers to any place value using real world applications.

Date: 6/28/13

1.C.36

Problem 1

Determine the best estimate to solve an application problem.

In the year 2012, there were 935,292 visitors to the White House.

T: Let's read together. Now, use this information to predict the number of White House maps needed for visitors in 2013. Discuss with your partner how you made your estimate.

S: I predict 940,000 maps are needed. I rounded to the nearest ten thousands place in order to make sure every visitor has a map. It is better to have more maps than not enough maps. → I predict more people may visit the White House in 2013. So I rounded to the nearest ten thousand— 940,000—the only estimate that is greater than the actual number.

T: (Display.) In the year 2011, there were 998,250 visitors to the White House. Discuss with your partner how this data may change your estimate.

S: The data shows the number of visitors has decreased in recent years. It may be wiser to predict 935,000 or 900,000 maps needed for 2013.

T: How can you determine the best estimate in a situation?

S: I can notice patterns or data that might inform my estimate.

NOTES ON MULTIPLE MEANS OF REPRESENTATION:

For ELL students, define unfamiliar words and experiences, such as the *White House*. Give an alternative example using a more familiar tourist attraction, perhaps from their cultural experience.

Problem 2

Choose the unit of rounding to solve an application problem.

T: (Display.) 2,837 students attend Lincoln Elementary school. Discuss with your partner how you would estimate the number of chairs needed in the school.

S: I would round to the nearest thousand for an estimate of 3,000 chairs needed. If I rounded to the nearest hundred—2,800—some students may not have a seat. → I disagree. 3,000 is almost 200 too many. I would round to the nearest hundred because some students might be absent.

T: Compare the effect of rounding to the largest unit in this problem and Problem 1.

S: In Problem 1, rounding to the largest unit resulted in a number less than the actual number. By contrast, when we rounded to the largest unit in Problem 2, our estimate was greater.

T: What can you conclude?

S: Rounding to the largest unit will effect different results for different numbers. → I will choose the unit based on the situation and what is most reasonable.

NOTES ON MULTIPLE MEANS OF ENGAGEMENT:

Challenge above grade level students to think of at least two situations similar to that of Problem 2 where choosing the unit to which to round is important to the outcome of the problem. Have them share and discuss.

$$2,837 \approx 3,000$$
$$2,837 \approx 2,800$$
$$2,837 \approx 2,840$$

Lesson 10:   Use place value understanding to round multi-digit numbers to any place value using real world applications.

Date: 6/28/13

1.C.37

Problem Set (10 minutes)

Students should do their personal best to complete the Problem Set within the allotted 10 minutes. For some classes, it may be appropriate to modify the assignment by specifying which problems they work on first. Some problems do not specify a method for solving. Students solve these problems using the RDW approach used for Application Problems.

Student Debrief (12 minutes)

Lesson Objective: Use place value understanding to round multi-digit numbers to any place value using real world applications.

Invite students to review their solutions for the Problem Set and the totality of the lesson experience. They should check work by comparing answers with a partner before going over answers as a class. Look for misconceptions or misunderstandings that can be addressed in the Debrief. Guide students in a conversation to debrief the Problem Set. You may choose to use any combination of the questions below to lead the discussion.

- In Problem 3 why didn't rounding to the nearest hundred work? Would rounding to the nearest thousand have worked better? What does this show you about rounding?

- When estimating, how do you choose to which unit you will round? Would it have been more difficult to solve Problem 5 if you rounded both numbers to the hundreds? Why or why not?

- Notice, in Problem 5, that 65,000 rounded to 70,000 and that 7,460 rounded to 7,000. What is the relationship between 7,000 and 70,000. How does this relationship make it easier to determine the number of trips?

- In Problem 1, how do your estimates compare?

- How do you choose a best estimate? What is the advantage of rounding to smaller and larger units?

- Why might you round up, even though the numbers tell you to round down?

NYS COMMON CORE MATHEMATICS CURRICULUM

Name __Jack_____   Date _____

1. Round 543,982 to the nearest:
    a. thousand: _544,000_____
    b. ten thousand: _540,000_____
    c. hundred thousand: _500,000_____

2. Complete each statement by rounding the number to the given place value.
    a. 2,841 rounded to the nearest hundred is _2,800_____.
    b. 32,851 rounded to the nearest hundred is _32,900_____.
    c. 132,891 rounded to the nearest hundred is _132,900_____.
    d. 6,299 rounded to the nearest thousand is _6,000_____.
    e. 36,599 rounded to the nearest thousand is _37,000_____.
    f. 100,699 rounded to the nearest thousand is _101,000_____.
    g. 40,984 rounded to the nearest ten thousand is _40,000_____.
    h. 54,984 rounded to the nearest ten thousand is _50,000_____.
    i. 997,010 rounded to the nearest ten thousand is _1,000,000_____.
    j. 360,034 rounded to the nearest hundred thousand is _400,000_____.
    k. 436,709 rounded to the nearest hundred thousand is _400,000_____.
    l. 1,852,442 rounded to the nearest hundred thousand is _1,900,000_____.

COMMON CORE   Lesson 10: Use place value understanding to round multi-digit numbers to any place value using real world applications   Date: 4/15/13   engage^ny   1.C.8

NYS COMMON CORE MATHEMATICS CURRICULUM

3. Empire Elementary School needs to purchase water bottles for field day. There are 2,142 students. Principal Vadar rounded to the nearest hundred to estimate how many water bottles to order. Will there be enough water bottles for everyone? Explain.

    2,142 ≈ 2,100

    There will not be enough water bottles because 2,142 rounded to the nearest hundred is 2,100. If Principal Vadar orders 2,100, there will be 42 students without water.

4. Opening day at the New York State Fair in 2012 had an attendance of 46,753. Decide which place value to round 46,753 to if you were writing a newspaper article. Round the number and explain why it is an appropriate unit to round the attendance to.

    I would round 46,753 to the ten thousands place to get 50,000. For a newspaper article, saying approximately 50,000 were in attendance is a nice round number that is pretty close to the actual number.

5. A jet air plane holds about 65,000 gallons of gas. It uses about 7,460 gallons when flying between New York City and Los Angeles. Round each number to the largest place value. Then find out about how many trips the plane can take between cities before running out of fuel?

    65,000 ≈ 70,000
    7,460 ≈ 7,000

    The plane can take about 10 trips between cities before running out of fuel because when I rounded, 70,000 is ten times as much as 7,000.

COMMON CORE   Lesson 10: Use place value understanding to round multi-digit numbers to any place value using real world applications   Date: 4/15/13   engage^ny   1.C.9

Lesson 10:   Use place value understanding to round multi-digit numbers to any place value using real world applications.
Date: 6/28/13

1.C.38

Exit Ticket (3 minutes)

After the Student Debrief, instruct students to complete the Exit Ticket. A review of their work will help you assess the students' understanding of the concepts that were presented in the lesson today and plan more effectively for future lessons. You may read the questions aloud to the students.

Lesson 10:   Use place value understanding to round multi-digit numbers to any place value using real world applications.

Date: 6/28/13

1.C.39

A

Correct _____

Round to the nearest ten thousand.

1	21,000 ≈			23	185,000 ≈	
2	31,000 ≈			24	85,000 ≈	
3	41,000 ≈			25	95,000 ≈	
4	541,000 =			26	97,000 ≈	
5	49,000 ≈			27	98,000 ≈	
6	59,000 ≈			28	198,000 ≈	
7	69,000 ≈			29	798,000 ≈	
8	369,000 ≈			30	31,200 ≈	
9	62,000 ≈			31	49,300 ≈	
10	712,000 ≈			32	649,300 ≈	
11	28,000 ≈			33	64,520 ≈	
12	37,000 ≈			34	164,520 ≈	
13	137,000 ≈			35	17,742 ≈	
14	44,000 ≈			36	917,742 ≈	
15	56,000 ≈			37	38,396 ≈	
16	456,000 ≈			38	64,501 ≈	
17	15,000 ≈			39	703,280 ≈	
18	25,000 ≈			40	239,500 ≈	
19	35,000 ≈			41	708,170 ≈	
20	235,000 ≈			42	188,631 ≈	
21	75,000 ≈			43	777,499 ≈	
22	175,000 ≈			44	444,919 ≈	

© Bill Davidson

Lesson 10:   Use place value understanding to round multi-digit numbers to
any place value using real world applications.

Date: 6/28/13

1.C.40

B   Improvement _____   # Correct _____

Round to the nearest ten thousand.

#	Problem	Answer	#	Problem	Answer
1	11,000 ≈		23	185,000 ≈	
2	21,000 ≈		24	85,000 ≈	
3	31,000 ≈		25	95,000 ≈	
4	531,000 =		26	96,000 ≈	
5	39,000 ≈		27	99,000 ≈	
6	49,000 ≈		28	199,000 ≈	
7	59,000 ≈		29	799,000 ≈	
8	359,000 ≈		30	21,200 ≈	
9	52,000 ≈		31	39,300 ≈	
10	612,000 ≈		32	639,300 ≈	
11	18,000 ≈		33	54,520 ≈	
12	27,000 ≈		34	154,520 ≈	
13	127,000 ≈		35	27,742 ≈	
14	34,000 ≈		36	927,742 ≈	
15	46,000 ≈		37	28,396 ≈	
16	346,000 ≈		38	54,501 ≈	
17	25,000 ≈		39	603,280 ≈	
18	35,000 ≈		40	139,500 ≈	
19	45,000 ≈		41	608,170 ≈	
20	245,000 ≈		42	177,631 ≈	
21	65,000 ≈		43	888,499 ≈	
22	165,000 ≈		44	444,909 ≈	

© Bill Davidson

COMMON CORE™   **Lesson 10:**   Use place value understanding to round multi-digit numbers to any place value using real world applications.   **1.C.41**

Date: 6/28/13

Name _____   Date _____

1. Round 543,982 to the nearest

    a. thousand: _____

    b. ten thousand: _____

    c. hundred thousand: _____

2. Complete each statement by rounding the number to the given place value.

    a.   2,841 rounded to the nearest hundred is _____.

    b.   32,851 rounded to the nearest hundred is _____.

    c.   132,891 rounded to the nearest hundred is _____.

    d.   6,299 rounded to the nearest thousand is _____.

    e.   36,599 rounded to the nearest thousand is _____.

    f.   100,699 rounded to the nearest thousand is _____.

    g.   40,984 rounded to the nearest ten thousand is _____.

    h.   54,984 rounded to the nearest ten thousand is _____.

    i.   997,010 rounded to the nearest ten thousand is _____.

    j.   360,034 rounded to the nearest hundred thousand is _____.

    k.   436,709 rounded to the nearest hundred thousand is _____.

    l.   1,852,442 rounded to the nearest hundred thousand is _____.

COMMON CORE™   Lesson 10:   Use place value understanding to round multi-digit numbers to
                                      any place value using real world applications.   1.C.42
                      Date: 6/28/13

3. Empire Elementary School needs to purchase water bottles for field day. There are 2,142 students. Principal Vadar rounded to the nearest hundred to estimate how many water bottles to order. Will there be enough water bottles for everyone? Explain.

4. Opening day at the New York State Fair in 2012 had an attendance of 46,753. Decide which place value to round 46,753 to if you were writing a newspaper article. Round the number and explain why it is an appropriate unit to round the attendance to.

5. A jet air plane holds about 65,000 gallons of gas. It uses about 7,460 gallons when flying between New York City and Los Angeles. Round each number to the largest place value. Then find out about how many trips the plane can take between cities before running out of fuel?

COMMON CORE™   Lesson 10:   Use place value understanding to round multi-digit numbers to any place value using real world applications.
Date: 6/28/13

© 2013 Common Core, Inc. All rights reserved. commoncore.org

1.C.43

Name _____   Date _____

1. There are 598,500 Apple employees in the United States.

   a. Round the number of employees to the given place value:

      thousand _____

      ten thousand _____

      hundred thousand _____

   b. Explain why two of your answers are the same.

2. A company developed a student survey so that students could share their thoughts about school. In 2011, 78,234 students across the United States were administered the survey. In 2012, the company planned to administer the survey to 10 times as many students from 2011. About how many surveys should the company have printed in 2012? Explain how you found your answer.

COMMON CORE™ | Lesson 10: | Use place value understanding to round multi-digit numbers to
any place value using real world applications.
Date: | 6/28/13 | 1.C.44

© 2013 Common Core, Inc. All rights reserved. commoncore.org

Name _____   Date _____

1. Round 845,001 to the nearest

   a. thousand: _____

   b. ten thousand: _____

   d. hundred thousand: _____

2. Complete each statement by rounding the number to the given place value.

   a. 783 rounded to the nearest hundred is _____.

   b. 12,781 rounded to the nearest hundred is _____.

   c. 951,194 rounded to the nearest hundred is _____.

   d. 1,258 rounded to the nearest thousand is _____.

   e. 65,124 rounded to the nearest thousand is _____.

   f. 99,451 rounded to the nearest thousand is _____.

   g. 60,488 rounded to the nearest ten thousand is _____.

   h. 80,801 rounded to the nearest ten thousand is _____.

   i. 897,100 rounded to the nearest ten thousand is _____.

   j. 880,005 rounded to the nearest hundred thousand is _____.

   k. 545,999 rounded to the nearest hundred thousand is _____.

   l. 689,114 rounded to the nearest hundred thousand is _____.

COMMON CORE   Lesson 10:   Use place value understanding to round multi-digit numbers to
                                 any place value using real world applications.   **1.C.45**
                   Date: 6/28/13

3. Solve the following problems using pictures, numbers, and words.

 a. In the 2011 New York City Marathon, 29,867 men finished the race and 16,928 women finished the race. Each finisher was given a t-shirt. About how many men's shirts were given away? About how many women's shirts were given away? Explain how you found your answers.

 b. In the 2010 New York City Marathon, 42,429 people finished the race and received a medal. Before the race, the medals had to be ordered. If you were the person in charge of ordering the medals and estimated how many to order by rounding, would you have ordered enough medals? Explain your thinking.

 c. In 2010, 28,357 of the finishers were men and 14,072 of the finishers were women. About how many more men finished the race than women? To determine your answer, did you round to the nearest ten thousand or thousand? Explain.

COMMON CORE   Lesson 10:   Use place value understanding to round multi-digit numbers to
Date: any place value using real world applications.
6/28/13

© 2013 Common Core, Inc. All rights reserved. commoncore.org

1.C.46

GRADE 4 • MODULE 1

Topic D

Multi-Digit Whole Number Addition

4.OA.3, 4.NBT.4, 4.NBT.1, 4.NBT.2

Focus Standard:	4.OA.3	Solve multistep word problems posed with whole numbers and having whole-number answers using the four operations, including problems in which remainders must be interpreted. Represent these problems using equations with a letter standing for the unknown quantity. Assess the reasonableness of answers using mental computation and estimation strategies including rounding.
	4.NBT.4	Fluently add and subtract multi-digit whole numbers using the standard algorithm.
Instructional Days:	2	
Coherence -Links from:	G3–M2	Place Value and Problem Solving with Units of Measure
-Links to:	G5–M1	Place Value and Decimal Fractions

Moving away from special strategies for addition, students develop fluency with the standard addition algorithm (**4.NBT.4**). Students compose larger units to add like base ten units, such as composing 10 hundreds to make 1 thousand and working across the numbers unit by unit (ones with ones, thousands with thousands). Recording of the regrouping occurs on the line under the addends as shown to the right. For example, in the ones column, students do not record the 0 in the ones column and the 1 above the tens column, instead students record 10, writing the 1 under the tens column and then a 0 in the ones column. Students practice and apply the algorithm in context of word problems and assess the reasonableness of their answers using rounding (**4.OA.3**). When using tape diagrams to model word problems, students use a variable to represent the unknown quantity.

$$
\begin{array}{r}
755,206 \\
+\ \ 89,814 \\
\hline
845,020
\end{array}
$$

A Teaching Sequence Towards Mastery of Multi-Digit Whole Number Addition

**Objective 1: Use place value understanding to fluently add multi-digit whole numbers using the standard addition algorithm and apply the algorithm to solve word problems using tape diagrams.
(Lesson 11)**

**Objective 2: Solve multi-step word problems using the standard addition algorithm modeled with tape diagrams and assess the reasonableness of answers using rounding.
(Lesson 12)**

Lesson 11

Objective: Use place value understanding to fluently add multi-digit whole numbers using the standard addition algorithm and apply the algorithm to solve word problems using tape diagrams.

Suggested Lesson Structure

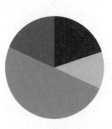

- ■ Fluency Practice   (12 minutes)
- ▨ Application Problem   (7 minutes)
- ■ Concept Development   (30 minutes)
- ■ Student Debrief   (11 minutes)
- **Total Time**   **(60 minutes)**

Fluency Practice (12 minutes)

- Round to Different Place Values **4.NBT.3**   (5 minutes)
- Multiply by 10 **4.NBT.1**   (4 minutes)
- Add Common Units **3.NBT.2**   (3 minutes)

Round to Different Place Values (5 minutes)

Materials: (S) Personal white boards

Note: This fluency reviews rounding skills that are building towards mastery.

T: (Write 3,941.) Say the number. We are going to round this number to the nearest thousand.
T: How many thousands are in 3,941?
S: 3 thousands.
T: (Label the lower endpoint of a vertical number line with 3,000.) And 1 more thousand will be?
S: 4 thousands.
T: (Mark the upper endpoint with 4,000.) Draw the same number line. (Students do so.)
T: What's halfway between 3,000 and 4,000?
S: 3,500.
T: Label 3,500 on your number line as I do the same. (Students do so.)
T: Label 3,941 on your number line. (Students do so.)
T: Is 3,941 nearer to 3,000 or 4,000?

Lesson 11: Use place value understanding to fluently add multi-digit whole numbers using the standard addition algorithm and apply the algorithm to solve word problems using tape diagrams.
Date: 6/28/13

© 2013 Common Core, Inc. All rights reserved. **commoncore.org**

1.D.2

T: (Write 3,941 ≈ _____.) Write your answer on your board.

S: (Students write 3,941 ≈ 4,000.)

Repeat process for 3,941 rounded to the nearest hundred, 74,621 rounded to the nearest ten thousand, and nearest thousand, 681,904 rounded to the nearest hundred thousand and nearest ten thousand, 681,904 rounded to the nearest thousand.

Multiply by 10 (4 minutes)

Materials: (S) Personal white boards

Note: This fluency will deepen student understanding of base ten units.

T: (Write 10 x _____ = 100.) Say the multiplication sentence.

S: 10 x 10 = 100.

T: (Write 10 x 1 ten = _____.) On your personal white boards, fill in the blank.

S: (Students write 10 x 1 ten = 10 tens.)

T: (Write 10 tens = _____ hundred.) On your personal white boards, fill in the blank.

T: (Write _____ ten x _____ ten = 1 hundred.) On your boards, fill in the blanks.

S: (Students write 1 ten x 1 ten = 1 hundred.)

Repeat process for the following possible sequence: 1 ten x 60 = _____, 1 ten x 30 = _____ hundreds, 1 ten x _____ = 900, 7 tens x 1 ten = _____ hundreds.

Note: Watch for students who say 3 tens x 4 tens is 12 tens rather than 12 hundreds.

Add Common Units (3 minutes)

Materials: (S) Personal white boards

Note: Reviewing this mental math fluency will prepare students for understanding the importance of the algorithm.

T: (Project 303.) Say the number in unit form.

S: 3 hundreds 3 ones.

T: (Write 303 + 202 = _____.) Say the addition sentence and answer in unit form.

S: 3 hundreds 3 ones + 2 hundreds 2 ones = 5 hundreds 5 ones.

T: Write the addition sentence on your personal white boards.

S: (Students write 303 + 202 = 505.)

Repeat process and sequence for 505 + 404; 5,005 + 5,004; 7,007 + 4,004; 8,008 + 5,005.

Lesson 11:   Use place value understanding to fluently add multi-digit whole
numbers using the standard addition algorithm and apply the
algorithm to solve word problems using tape diagrams.

Date: 6/28/13

1.D.3

Application Problem (7 minutes)

Meredith kept track of the calories she consumed for 3 weeks. The first week, she consumed 12,490 calories, the second week 14,295 calories, and the third week 11,116 calories. About how many calories did Meredith consume altogether? Which of these estimates will produce a more accurate answer: rounding to the nearest thousand or rounding to the nearest ten thousand? Explain.

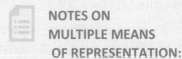

NOTES ON
MULTIPLE MEANS
OF REPRESENTATION:

For the application problem, students working below grade level may need further guidance in putting together three addends. Help them to break it down by putting two addends together and then adding the third addend to the total. Use manipulatives to demonstrate.

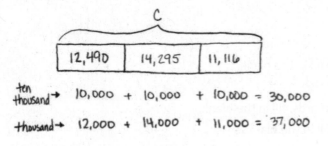

ten thousand → 10,000 + 10,000 + 10,000 = 30,000

thousand → 12,000 + 14,000 + 11,000 = 37,000

My 2 estimates are so far apart! But rounding to a smaller unit will always make the estimate closer to the actual answer. So Meredith consumed about 37,000 calories.

Note: This problem reviews rounding from Lesson 10, but can be used as an extension after the Debrief to support the objective of this lesson.

Concept Development (30 minutes)

Materials: (S) Personal white boards

Problem 1

Add, renaming once using disks in a place value chart.

  T: (Project vertically: 3,134 + 2,493.) Say this problem with me.
  S: Three thousand, one hundred thirty-four plus two thousand, four hundred ninety-three.
  T: Draw a tape diagram to represent this problem. What are the two parts that make up the whole?
  S: 3,134 and 2,493.
  T: Record that in the tape diagram.
  T: What is the unknown?
  S: In this case, the unknown is the whole.

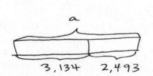

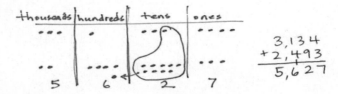

Lesson 11: Use place value understanding to fluently add multi-digit whole numbers using the standard addition algorithm and apply the algorithm to solve word problems using tape diagrams.

Date: 6/28/13

1.D.4

T: Show the whole above the tape diagram using a bracket and label the unknown quantity with the **variable** of a.

T: Draw disks into the place value chart to represent the first part, 3,134. Now, it's your turn. When you are done, add 2,493 by drawing more disks into your place value chart.

T: (Point to the problem.) 4 ones plus 3 ones equals?

S: 7 ones. (Count 7 ones in the chart and record 7 ones in the problem.)

T: (Point to the problem.) 3 tens plus 9 tens equals?

S: 12 tens. (Count 12 tens in the chart.)

T: We can bundle 10 tens as 1 hundred. (Circle 10 ten disks, draw an arrow to the hundreds place and the 1 hundred disk to show the regrouping.)

T: We can represent this in writing. (Write 12 tens as 1 hundred, crossing the line, and 2 tens in the tens column, so that you are writing 12 and not 2 and 1 as separate numbers. Refer to the vertical equation visual above.)

T: (Point to the problem.) 1 hundred plus 4 hundreds plus 1 hundred equals?

S: 6 hundreds. (Count 6 hundreds in the chart, and record 6 hundreds in the problem.)

T: (Point to the problem.) 3 thousands plus 2 thousands equals?

S: 5 thousands. (Count 5 thousands in the chart, and record 5 thousands in the problem.)

T: Say the whole equation with me: 3,134 plus 2,493 equals 5,627. Label the whole in the tape diagram, above the bracket, with $a = 5{,}627$.

Problem 2

Add, renaming in multiple units using the standard algorithm and the place value chart.

T: (Project vertically: 40,762 + 30,473.)

T: With your partner, draw a tape diagram to model this problem labeling the two known parts and the unknown whole, using B to represent the whole.

Circulate and assist students.

T: With your partner, write the problem and draw disks for the first addend in your chart. Then, draw disks for the second addend.

T: (Point to the problem.) 2 ones plus 3 ones equals?

S: 5 ones. (Students count the disks to confirm 5 ones and write 5 in the ones column.)

T: 6 tens plus 7 tens equals?

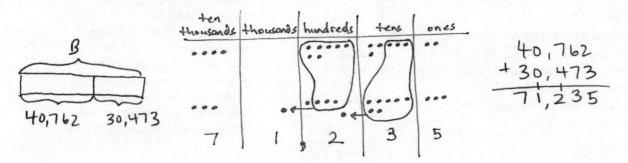

Lesson 11:   Use place value understanding to fluently add multi-digit whole numbers using the standard addition algorithm and apply the algorithm to solve word problems using tape diagrams.
Date: 6/28/13

1.D.5

S: 13 tens. → We can group 10 tens to make 1 hundred. → We don't write two digits in one column. We can change 10 tens for 1 hundred leaving us with 3 tens.

T: (Regroup the disks.) Watch me as I record the larger unit using the addition **algorithm**.

First, record the 1 below the digits in the hundreds place then record the 3 in the tens, so that you are writing 13, not 3 then 1.

T: 7 hundreds plus 4 hundreds plus 1 hundred equals 12 hundreds. Discuss with your partner how to record this.

Continue adding, regrouping, and recording across other units.

T: Say the whole equation with me. 40,762 plus 30,473 equals 71,235. Label the whole in the bar diagram with 71,235, and write B = 71,235.

Problem 3

Add, renaming multiple units using the standard algorithm.

T: (Project: 207,426 + 128,744.)

T: Draw a tape diagram to model this problem. Record the numbers on your board.

T: With your partner, add units right to left, regrouping when necessary using the addition algorithm.

S: 207,426 + 128,744 = 336,170.

$$\begin{array}{r} 207,426 \\ +\,128,744 \\ \hline 336,170 \end{array}$$

Problem 4

Solve one-step word problem using standard algorithm modeled with a tape diagram.

The Lane family took a road trip. During the first week, they drove 907 miles. The second week they drove the same amount as the first week plus an additional 297 miles. How many miles did they drive during the second week?

T: What information do we know?

S: We know they drove 907 miles the first week. We also know they drove 297 miles more during the second week than the first week.

T: What is the unknown information?

S: We don't know the total miles they drove in the second week.

T: Draw a tape diagram to represent the amount of miles in the first week, 907 miles. Since the Lane family drove an additional 297 miles in the second week, extend the bar for 297 more miles. What does the bar represent?

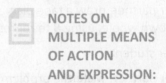

NOTES ON MULTIPLE MEANS OF ACTION AND EXPRESSION:

ELLs benefit from further explanation of the word problem. Have a conversation around the following: "What do we do if we don't understand a word in the problem? What thinking can we use to figure out the answer anyway?"

In this case, students do not need to know what a road trip is in order to solve. Discuss, "How is the tape diagram helpful to us?" It may be helpful to use the RDW approach: Read important information, draw a picture, and write an equation to solve.

Lesson 11:   Use place value understanding to fluently add multi-digit whole numbers using the standard addition algorithm and apply the algorithm to solve word problems using tape diagrams.

Date: 6/28/13

S: The number of miles they drove in the second week.

T: Use a bracket to label the unknown as *M* for miles.

T: How do we solve for M?

S: 907 + 297 = M. (Check student algorithms to see they are recording the regrouping of 10 of a smaller unit for 1 larger unit.)

T: Solve. What is M?

S: M equals 1,204. (Write M = 1,204.)

T: Write a sentence that tells your answer.

S: The Lane family drove 1,204 miles during the second week.

Problem Set (10 minutes)

Students should do their personal best to complete the Problem Set within the allotted 10 minutes. For some classes, it may be appropriate to modify the assignment by specifying which problems they work on first. Some problems do not specify a method for solving. Students solve these problems using the RDW approach used for Application Problems.

Student Debrief (11 minutes)

Lesson Objective: Use place value understanding to fluently add multi-digit whole numbers using the standard addition algorithm and apply the algorithm to solve word problems using tape diagrams.

Invite students to review their solutions for the Problem Set and the totality of the lesson experience. They should check work by comparing answers with a partner before going over answers as a class. Look for misconceptions or misunderstandings that can be addressed in the Debrief. Guide students in a conversation to debrief the Problem Set. You may choose to use any combination of the questions below to lead the discussion.

- When we are writing a sentence to express our answer, what part of the original problem helps us to tell our answer using the correct words and context?

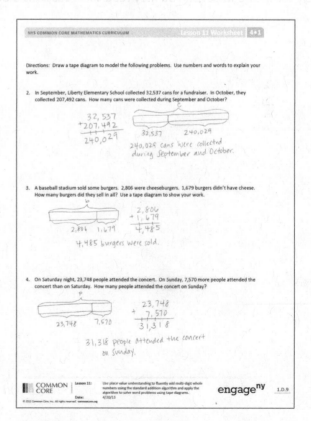

Lesson 11:   Use place value understanding to fluently add multi-digit whole numbers using the standard addition algorithm and apply the algorithm to solve word problems using tape diagrams.

Date: 6/28/13

1.D.7

© 2013 Common Core, Inc. All rights reserved. **commoncore.org**

- What purpose does a tape diagram have? How does it support your work?

- What does a **variable**, like the letter *B* in Problem 2, help us do when drawing a tape diagram?

- I see different types of tape diagrams drawn for Problem 3. Some drew one bar with two parts. Some drew one bar for each addend, and put the bracket for the whole on the right side of both bars. Will these diagrams result in different answers? Explain.

- In Problem 1, what did you notice was similar and different about the addends and the sums for Parts (a), (b), and (c)?

- If you have 2 addends, can you ever have enough ones to make 2 tens, or enough tens to make 2 hundreds, or enough hundreds to make 2 thousands? Try it out with your partner. What if you have 3 addends?

- In Problem 1, each unit used the numbers 2, 5, and 7 once, but the sum doesn't show repeating digits. Why not?

- How is recording the regrouped number in the next column of the addition **algorithm** related to bundling disks?

- Have students revisit the Application Problem and solve for the actual amount of calories consumed. Which unit when rounding provided an estimate closer to the actual value?

Exit Ticket (3 minutes)

After the Student Debrief, instruct students to complete the Exit Ticket. A review of their work will help you assess the students' understanding of the concepts that were presented in the lesson today and plan more effectively for future lessons. You may read the questions aloud to the students.

Name _____   Date _____

1. Solve the addition problems below using the standard algorithm.

   a.   6, 3 1 1

        +   2 6 8

   b.   6, 3 1 1

        + 1, 2 6 8

   c.   6, 3 1 4

        +   1, 2 6 8

   d.   6, 3 1 4

        + 2, 4 9 3

   e.   8, 3 1 4

        + 2, 4 9 3

   f.   1 2, 3 7 8

        +   5, 4 6 3

   g.   5 2, 0 9 8

        +   6, 0 4 8

   h.   3 4, 6 9 8

        + 7 1, 8 4 0

   i.   5 4 4, 8 1 1

        + 3 5 6, 4 4 5

   j.   527 + 275 + 752 =

   k.   38,193 + 6,376 + 241,457 =

COMMON CORE™   Lesson 11:   Use place value understanding to fluently add multi-digit whole numbers using the standard addition algorithm and apply the algorithm to solve word problems using tape diagrams.   1.D.9

Date: 6/28/13

Directions: Draw a tape diagram to model the following problems. Use numbers and words to explain your work.

2. In September, Liberty Elementary School collected 32,537 cans for a fundraiser. In October, they collected 207,492 cans. How many cans were collected during September and October?

3. A baseball stadium sold some burgers: 2,806 were cheeseburgers and 1,679 burgers didn't have cheese. How many burgers did they sell in all? Use a tape diagram to show your work.

4. On Saturday night, 23,748 people attended the concert. On Sunday, 7,570 more people attended the concert than on Saturday. How many people attended the concert on Sunday?

COMMON CORE™ | **Lesson 11:** Use place value understanding to fluently add multi-digit whole numbers using the standard addition algorithm and apply the algorithm to solve word problems using tape diagrams.

Date: 6/28/13

© 2013 Common Core, Inc. All rights reserved. **commoncore.org**

1.D.10

Name _____   Date _____

1. Find the sums of the following:

   a.   2 3, 6 0 7
       + 2, 3 0 7

   b.   3, 9 4 8
       +   2 7 8

   c.   5,983 + 2,097

2. The office supply closet had 25,473 large paperclips, 13,648 medium paperclips, and 15,306 small paperclips. How many paperclips were in the closet?

COMMON CORE™

Lesson 11: Use place value understanding to fluently add multi-digit whole numbers using the standard addition algorithm and apply the algorithm to solve word problems using tape diagrams.

Date: 6/28/13

1.D.11

© 2013 Common Core, Inc. All rights reserved. **commoncore.org**

Name _____   Date _____

1. Solve the addition problems below using the standard algorithm.

a.   7,909
       +1,044

b.   27,909
       +9,740

c.   827,909
      +42,989

d.   289,205
      +11,845

e.   547,982
     +114,849

f.   258,983
     +121,897

g.   83,906
      +35,808

h.   289,999
      +91,849

i.   754,900
     +245,100

COMMON CORE™   **Lesson 11:**   Use place value understanding to fluently add multi-digit whole numbers using the standard addition algorithm and apply the algorithm to solve word problems using tape diagrams.   **1.D.12**

Date: 6/28/13

Directions: Draw a tape diagram to model the following problem. Use numbers and words to explain your work.

2. At the zoo, Brooke learned that one of rhinos weighed 4,897 pounds, one of the giraffes weighed 2,667 pounds, one of the African elephants weighed 12,456 pounds, and one of the Komodo dragons weighed 123 pounds.

    a. What is the combined weight of the zoo's African elephant and the giraffe?

    b. What is the combined weight of the zoo's African elephant and the rhino?

    c. What is the combined weight of the zoo's African elephant, the rhino, and the giraffe?

    d. What is the combined weight of the zoo's Komodo dragon and the rhino?

Lesson 11:   Use place value understanding to fluently add multi-digit whole
                numbers using the standard addition algorithm and apply the
Date: algorithm to solve word problems using tape diagrams.
                6/28/13

1.D.13

Lesson 12

Objective: Solve multi-step word problems using the standard addition algorithm modeled with tape diagrams and assess the reasonableness of answers using rounding.

Suggested Lesson Structure

■ Fluency Practice   (12 minutes)
■ Application Problems   (5 minutes)
■ Concept Development   (34 minutes)
■ Student Debrief   (9 minutes)
   Total Time   **(60 minutes)**

Fluency Practice (12 minutes)

▪ Round to Different Place Values **4.NBT.3**   (6 minutes)
▪ Find the Sum **4.NBT.4**   (6 minutes)

Round to Different Place Values (6 minutes)

Materials: (S) Personal white boards

Note: This fluency reviews rounding skills that are building towards mastery.

   T: (Project 726,354.) Say the number.
   S: Seven hundred twenty-six thousand, three hundred fifty-four.
   T: What digit is in the hundred thousands place?
   S: 7.
   T: What's the value of the digit 7?
   S: 700,000.
   T: On your personal white boards, round the number to the nearest hundred thousand.
   S: (Students write 726,354 ≈ 700,000.)

Repeat process, rounding 726,354 to the nearest ten thousand, thousand, hundred, and ten. Follow the same process and sequence for 496,517.

Lesson 12:   Solve multi-step word problems using the standard addition algorithm modeled with tape diagrams and assess the reasonableness of answers using rounding.
Date: 6/28/13

1.D.14

Find the Sum (6 minutes)

Materials: (S) Personal white boards

Note: Reviewing this mental math fluency will prepare students for understanding the importance of the algorithm.

- T: (Write 417 + 232 =____.) Solve mentally or by writing horizontally or vertically.
- S: (Students write 417 + 232 = 649.)

Repeat process and sequence for 7073 + 2312; 13,705 + 4,412; 3,949 + 451; 538 + 385 + 853; and 23,944 + 6,056 + 159,368.

Application Problem (5 minutes)

The basketball team raised a total of $154,694 in September and $29,987 more in October than in September. How much money did they raise in October? Draw a tape diagram and write your answer in a complete sentence.

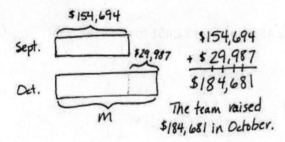

$154,694
+ $29,987
$184,681

The team raised $184,681 in October.

Note: This Application Problem reviews the addition algorithm practiced in yesterday's lesson by solving a comparative word problem.

Concept Development (34 minutes)

Problem 1

Solve a multi-step word problem using a tape diagram.

The city flower shop sold 14,594 pink roses on Valentine's Day. They sold 7,857 more red roses than pink roses. How many pink and red roses did the city flower shop sell altogether on Valentine's Day? Use a tape diagram to show your work.

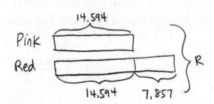

COMMON CORE™

Lesson 12:   Solve multi-step word problems using the standard addition algorithm modeled with tape diagrams and assess the reasonableness of answers using rounding.
Date: 6/28/13

1.D.15

T: Read the problem with me. What information do we know?

S: We know there are 14,594 pink roses sold.

T: To model this, let's draw one bar to represent the pink roses. Do we know how many red roses were sold?

S: No, but we know that there were 7,857 more red roses sold than pink roses.

T: A second bar can represent the number of red roses sold. (Model on tape diagram.)

T: What is the problem asking us to find?

S: The total number of roses.

T: We can draw a bracket to the side of both bars. Let's label it *R* for pink and red roses.

T: First, solve to find how many red roses were sold.

S: (Students solve 14,594 + 7,857 = 22,451.)

MP.2

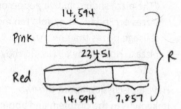

T: What does the bottom bar represent?

S: The bottom bar represents the number of red roses, 22,451. (Bracket 22,451 to show the total number of red roses.)

T: Now we need to find the total number of roses sold.

T: How do we solve for R?

S: Add the totals for both bars together. 14,594 + 22,451 = R.

T: Solve with me. What does R equal?

S: R equals 37,045. (Write R = 37,045.)

T: Let's write a statement of the answer.

S: The city flower shop sold 37,045 pink and red roses on Valentine's Day.

Problem 2

Solve a two-step word problem using a tape diagram and assess the reasonableness of the answer.

On Saturday, 32,736 more bus tickets were sold than on Sunday. On Sunday, only 17,295 tickets were sold. How many people bought bus tickets over the weekend? Use a tape diagram to show your work.

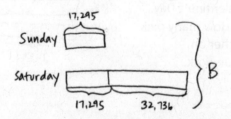

COMMON CORE™

Lesson 12: Solve multi-step word problems using the standard addition algorithm modeled with tape diagrams and assess the reasonableness of answers using rounding.

Date: 6/28/13

1.D.16

T: Tell your partner what information we know.

S: We know how many people bought bus tickets on Sunday, 17,295. We also know how many more people bought tickets on Saturday. But we don't know the total number of people that bought tickets on Saturday.

T: Let's draw a bar for Sunday's ticket sales and label it. How can we represent Saturday's ticket sales?

S: Draw a bar the same length as Sunday's and extend it further for 32,736 more tickets.

T: What does the problem ask us to solve for?

S: The number of people that bought tickets over the weekend.

T: With your partner, finish drawing a tape diagram to model this problem. Use *B* to represent the total number of tickets bought over the weekend.

T: Before we solve, estimate to get a general sense of what our answer will be. Round each number to the nearest ten thousand.

S: 20,000 + 20,000 + 30,000 = 70,000. About 70,000 tickets were sold over the weekend.

T: Now solve with your partner to find the actual number of tickets sold over the weekend.

S: (Students solve.)

S: B equals 67,326. (Write B = 67,326.)

T: Now let's look back at the estimate we got earlier and compare with our actual answer. Is 67,326 close to 70,000?

S: Yes, 67,326 rounded to the nearest ten thousand is 70,000.

T: Our answer is reasonable.

T: Write a statement of the answer.

S: There were 67,326 people who bought bus tickets over the weekend.

Problem 3

Solve a multi-step word problem using a tape diagram and assess reasonableness.

Last year, Big Bill's Department Store sold many pairs of shoes: 118,214 pairs of boots were sold; 37,092 more pairs of sandals than pairs of boots were sold; and 124,417 more pairs of sneakers than pairs of boots were sold. How many pairs of shoes were sold last year?

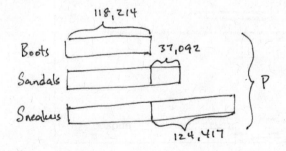

$$118,214 + 37,092$$
sandals = 155,306

$$118,214 + 124,417$$
sneakers = 242631

$$155,306 \\ 242,631 \\ + 118,214 \\ \hline 516,151 = S$$

516,151 pairs of shoes were sold last year.

COMMON CORE™

Lesson 12:   Solve multi-step word problems using the standard addition algorithm modeled with tape diagrams and assess the reasonableness of answers using rounding.

Date: 6/28/13

1.D.17

T: Discuss with your partner the information we have and the unknown information we want to find.

S: (Students discuss.)

T: With your partner, draw a tape diagram to model this problem. How do you solve for *P*?

S: The bar shows me I could add the number of pairs of boots 3 times then add 37,092 and 124,417. → You could find the number of pairs of sandals, find the number of pairs of sneakers, and then add those totals to the number of pairs of boots.

Have the students then round each addend to get an estimated answer, calculate precisely, and compare to see if their answer is reasonable.

Problem Set (10 minutes)

Students should do their personal best to complete the Problem Set within the allotted 10 minutes. For some classes, it may be appropriate to modify the assignment

by specifying which problems they work on first. Some problems do not specify a method for solving. Students solve these problems using the RDW approach used for Application Problems.

Student Debrief (9 minutes)

Lesson Objective: Solve multi-step word problems using the standard addition algorithm modeled with tape diagrams and assess the reasonableness of answers using rounding.

The Student Debrief is intended to invite reflection and active processing of the total lesson experience.

Invite students to review their solutions for the Problem Set. They should check work by comparing answers with a partner before going over answers as a class. Look for misconceptions or misunderstandings that can be addressed in the Debrief. Guide students in a conversation to debrief the Problem Set and process the lesson. You may choose to use any combination of the questions below to lead the discussion.

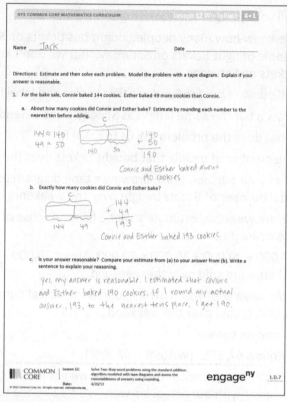

Lesson 12: Solve multi-step word problems using the standard addition algorithm modeled with tape diagrams and assess the reasonableness of answers using rounding.

Date: 6/28/13

© 2013 Common Core, Inc. All rights reserved. commoncore.org

1.D.18

- Explain why we should test to see if our answers are reasonable. (Show an example of one of the above CD problems solved incorrectly to show how checking the reasonableness of an answer is important.)
- When might you need to use an estimate in real life?
- Let's check the reasonableness of our answer in the Application Problem.
  - Allow half of the class to round to the nearest hundred thousand. Others may round to the nearest ten thousand.
  - Note that rounding to the ten thousands brings our estimate closer to the actual answer.
  - Note that the round to the nearest hundred thousand estimate is nearly 60,000 less than the actual answer.
  - Discuss the margin of error that occurs in estimating answers and how this relates to the place value to which you round.
- Problem 1
  - How would your estimate be affected if you rounded all numbers to the nearest hundred?
  - What are the next steps if your estimate is not near the actual answer? Consider the example we discussed earlier where the problem was solved incorrectly, but because there was an estimated answer, we knew our answer was not reasonable.

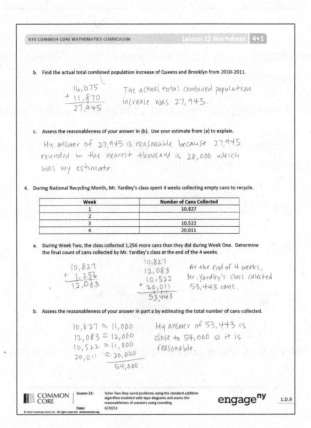

Exit Ticket (3 minutes)

After the Student Debrief, instruct students to complete the Exit Ticket. A review of their work will help you assess the students' understanding of the concepts that were presented in the lesson today and plan more effectively for future lessons. You may read the questions aloud to the students.

Lesson 12: Solve multi-step word problems using the standard addition algorithm modeled with tape diagrams and assess the reasonableness of answers using rounding.

Date: 6/28/13

Name _____   Date _____

Directions: Estimate and then solve each problem. Model the problem with a tape diagram. Explain if your answer is reasonable.

1. For the bake sale, Connie baked 144 cookies. Esther baked 49 more cookies than Connie.

   a. About how many cookies did Connie and Esther bake? Estimate by rounding each number to the nearest ten before adding.

   b. Exactly how many cookies did Connie and Esther bake?

   c. Is your answer reasonable? Compare your estimate from (a) to your answer from (b). Write a sentence to explain your reasoning.

Lesson 12:   Solve multi-step word problems using the standard addition algorithm modeled with tape diagrams and assess the reasonableness of answers using rounding.

Date: 6/28/13

© 2013 Common Core, Inc. All rights reserved. commoncore.org

1.D.20

2. Raffle tickets were sold for a school fundraiser to parents, teachers, and students. 563 tickets were sold to teachers. 888 more tickets were sold to students than to teachers. 904 tickets were sold to parents. How many tickets were sold to parents, teachers, and students?

   a. About how many tickets were sold to parents, teachers, and students? Round each number to the nearest hundred to find your estimate.

   b. Exactly how many tickets were sold to parents, teachers, and students?

   c. Assess the reasonableness of your answer in (b). Use your estimate from (a) to explain.

3. From 2010 to 2011, the population of Queens increased by 16,075. Brooklyn's population increased by 11,870 more than the population increase of Queens.

   a. Estimate the total combined population increase of Queens and Brooklyn from 2010 to 2011. (Round the addends to estimate.)

Lesson 12:   Solve multi-step word problems using the standard addition algorithm
modeled with tape diagrams and assess the reasonableness of
answers using rounding.
Date: 6/28/13   1.D.21

b. Find the actual total combined population increase of Queens and Brooklyn from 2010 to 2011.

c. Assess the reasonableness of your answer in (b). Use your estimate from (a) to explain.

4. During National Recycling Month, Mr. Yardley's class spent 4 weeks collecting empty cans to recycle.

Week	Number of Cans Collected
1	10,827
2	
3	10,522
4	20,011

a. During Week 2, the class collected 1,256 more cans than they did during Week 1.
Determine the final count of cans collected by Mr. Yardley's class at the end of the 4 weeks.

b. Assess the reasonableness of your answer in part a by estimating the total number of cans collected.

Lesson 12:   Solve multi-step word problems using the standard addition algorithm
                modeled with tape diagrams and assess the reasonableness of
                answers using rounding.
Date: 6/28/13

1.D.22

Name _____   Date _____

Directions: Model the problem with a tape diagram. Solve and write your answer as a statement.

1. In January, Scott earned $8,999. In February, he earned $2,387 more than he did in January. In March, Scott earned the same amount as he did in February. How much did Scott earn altogether during those three months? Is your answer reasonable? Explain.

Lesson 12:   Solve multi-step word problems using the standard addition algorithm
            modeled with tape diagrams and assess the reasonableness of
            answers using rounding.
Date: 6/28/13

1.D.23

Name _____   Date _____

Directions: Estimate and then solve each problem. Model the problem with a tape diagram. Explain if your answer is reasonable.

1. There were 3,905 more hits on the school's website in January than February. February had 9,854 hits. How many hits did the school's website have during both months?

   a. About how many hits did the website have during January and February?

   b. Exactly how many hits did the website have during January and February?

   c. Is your answer reasonable? Compare your estimate from (a) to your answer from (b). Write a sentence to explain your reasoning.

2. On Sunday, 77,098 fans attended a New York Jets football game. The same day 3,397 more fans attended a New York Giants game than the Jets game. How many football fans watched the Jets and Giants play on Sunday?

   a. What was the actual number of fans who watched the games?

   b. Is your answer reasonable? Round each number to the nearest thousand to find an estimate of how many fans there are.

Lesson 12:	Solve multi-step word problems using the standard addition algorithm modeled with tape diagrams and assess the reasonableness of answers using rounding.
Date:	6/28/13

1.D.24

3. Last year on Ted's farm, his four cows produced the following liters of milk:

Cow	Liters of Milk Produced
Daisy	5,098
Betsy	
Mary	9,980
Buttercup	7,087

a. Betsy produced 986 more liters of milk than Buttercup. How many liters of milk did all 4 cows produce?

b. Is your answer reasonable? Explain.

Lesson 12:   Solve multi-step word problems using the standard addition algorithm modeled with tape diagrams and assess the reasonableness of answers using rounding.

Date: 6/28/13

1.D.25

Topic E
Multi-Digit Whole Number Subtraction

4.OA.3, 4.NBT.4, 4.NBT.1, 4.NBT.2

Focus Standard:	4.OA.3	Solve multistep word problems posed with whole numbers and having whole-number answers using the four operations, including problems in which remainders must be interpreted. Represent these problems using equations with a letter standing for the unknown quantity. Assess the reasonableness of answers using mental computation and estimation strategies including rounding.
	4.NBT.4	Fluently add and subtract multi-digit whole numbers using the standard algorithm.
Instructional Days:	4	
Coherence -Links from:	G3–M2	Place Value and Problem Solving with Units of Measure
-Links to:	G5–M1	Place Value and Decimal Fractions

Following the introduction of the standard algorithm for addition in Topic D, the standard algorithm for subtraction replaces special strategies for subtraction in Topic E. Moving slowly from smaller to larger minuends, students practice decomposing larger units into smaller units. First, only one decomposition is introduced, where one zero may appear in the minuend. Students continue to decompose all necessary digits before performing the algorithm, allowing subtraction from left to right, or as taught in the lessons from right to left. Students gain fluency in the algorithm to subtract numbers from 1 million allowing for multiple decompositions (**4.NBT.4**). The topic will conclude with practicing the standard subtraction algorithm in the context of two-step word problems where students will have to assess the reasonableness of their answers by rounding (**4.OA.3**). When using tape diagrams to model word problems, students use a variable to represent the unknown quantity.

$$
\begin{array}{r}
\overset{3}{\cancel{4}}\,\overset{11}{\cancel{2}}\,\overset{9}{\cancel{0}}\,\overset{10}{\cancel{0}}\,\overset{5}{6}\,\overset{11}{\cancel{1}} \\
4\,2\,0{,}0\,6\,1 \\
-\ \ 5\,6{,}3\,2\,8 \\
\hline
3\,6\,3{,}7\,3\,3
\end{array}
$$

A Teaching Sequence Towards Mastery of Multi-Digit Whole Number Subtraction

Objective 1: Use place value understanding to decompose to smaller units once using the standard subtraction algorithm, and apply the algorithm to solve word problems using tape diagrams.
(Lesson 13)

Objective 2: Use place value understanding to decompose to smaller units up to 3 times using the standard subtraction algorithm, and apply the algorithm to solve word problems using tape diagrams.
(Lesson 14)

Objective 3: Use place value understanding to fluently decompose to smaller units multiple times in any place using the standard subtraction algorithm, and apply the algorithm to solve word problems using tape diagrams.
(Lesson 15)

Objective 4: Solve two-step word problems using the standard subtraction algorithm fluently modeled with tape diagrams and assess the reasonableness of answers using rounding.
(Lesson 16)

Lesson 13

Objective: Use place value understanding to decompose to smaller units once using the standard subtraction algorithm and apply the algorithm to solve word problems using tape diagrams.

Suggested Lesson Structure

■ Fluency Practice   (12 minutes)
■ Application Problems   (5 minutes)
■ Concept Development   (35 minutes)
■ Student Debrief   (8 minutes)
  Total Time   **(60 minutes)**

Fluency Practice (12 minutes)

▪ Find the Sum **4.NBT.4**   (6 minutes)
▪ Subtract Common Units **4.NBT.3**   (6 minutes)

Find the Sum (6 minutes)

Materials: (S) Personal white boards

Note: Reviewing this mental math fluency will prepare students for understanding the importance of the addition algorithm.

    T: (Write 316 + 473 = ____.) Write an addition sentence horizontally or vertically.

    S: (Students write 316 + 473 = 789.)

Repeat process and sequence for 6,065 + 3,731; 13,806 + 4,393; 5,928 + 124; and 629 + 296 + 962.

Subtract Common Units (6 minutes)

Materials: (S) Personal white boards

Note: Reviewing this mental math fluency will prepare students for understanding the importance of the subtraction algorithm.

    T: (Project 707.) Say the number in unit form.

    S: 7 hundreds 7 ones.

    T: (Write 707 – 202 = ____.) Say the subtraction sentence and answer in unit form.

| Lesson 13: | Use place value understanding to decompose to smaller units once using the standard subtraction algorithm, and apply the algorithm to solve word problems using tape diagrams. | 1.E.3 |
| Date: | 6/28/13 | |

S: 7 hundreds 7 ones – 2 hundreds 2 ones = 5 hundreds 5 ones.

T: Write the subtraction sentence on your personal white boards.

S: (Students write 707 – 202 = 505.)

Repeat process and sequence for 909 – 404; 9,009 – 5,005; 11,011 – 4,004; and 13,013 – 8,008.

Application Problems (5 minutes)

Jennifer texted 5,849 times in January. In February, she texted 1,263 more times than she did in January. What was the total number of texts that Jennifer sent in the two months combined? Explain how you would check the reasonableness of your answer.

$$\begin{array}{ll} 5,849 & 7,112 \\ +\ 1,263 & +\ 5,849 \\ \hline 7,112 & 12,961 \end{array}$$

January ≈ 6,000 } 13,000
February ≈ 7,000

My answer is reasonable because if I round January and February, I get 13,000. 12,961 rounded is 13,000, so my answer is reasonable.

Jennifer sent 12,961 texts in January and February.

Note: This Application Problem reviews content from the previous lesson of a multi-step addition problem.

Concept Development (35 minutes)

Materials: (T) Place value chart, disks (S) Personal white board, place value charts, disks

Problem 1

Use a place value chart and disks to model subtracting alongside the algorithm, regrouping 1 hundred into 10 tens.

T: Write 4,259 – 2,171 vertically on the board.

T: Say this problem with me.

T: Watch as I draw a tape diagram to represent this problem. What is the whole?

S: 4,259.

T: We record that above the bar as the whole, and record the known part of 2,171 under the bar. Your turn to draw a tape diagram. Mark the unknown part of the diagram as A.

T: Model the whole, 4,259, using number disks on your place value chart.

T: Do we model the part we are subtracting?

S: No, just the total.

Lesson 13:   Use place value understanding to decompose to smaller units once using the standard subtraction algorithm, and apply the algorithm to solve word problems using tape diagrams.

Date: 6/28/13

© 2013 Common Core, Inc. All rights reserved. commoncore.org

1.E.4

T: First let's determine if we are ready to subtract. We look across the top number, from right to left, to see if there are enough units in each column. Is the number of units in the top number of the ones column greater than or equal to that of the bottom number? (Point to the 9 and the 1 in the equation.)

S: Yes, 9 is greater than 1.

T: That means we are ready to subtract in the ones column. Is the number of units in the top number of the tens column greater than or equal to that of the bottom number?

S: No, 5 is less than 7.

T: (Show regrouping on the place value chart.) We ungroup or unbundle 1 unit from the hundreds to make 10 tens. I now have 1 hundred and 15 tens. Let's represent the change in writing. (Cross out the hundreds and tens to rename them in the equation.)

T: Show the change with your disks. (Students cross off 1 hundred and change it for 10 tens as shown below.)

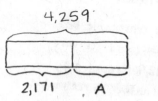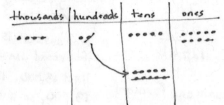

T: Is the number of units in the top number of the hundreds column greater than or equal to that of the bottom number?

S: Yes, 1 is equal to 1.

T: Is the number of units in the top number of the thousands column greater than or equal to that of the bottom number?

S: Yes, 4 is greater than 2.

T: Are we ready to subtract?

S: Yes, we are ready to subtract!

T: (Point to the algorithm.) 9 ones minus 1 one?

S: 8 ones. (Remove 1 disk; write an 8 in the algorithm.)

T: 15 tens minus 7 tens?

S: 8 tens. (Remove 7 disks; write an 8 in the algorithm.)

Continue subtracting through the hundreds and thousands.

T: Say the complete number sentence. (Read 4,259 – 2,171 = 2,088 together.)

T: The value of the A in our tape diagram is 2,088. We write A = 2,088 below the tape diagram. What can be added to 2,171 to result in the sum of 4,259?

S: 2,088.

Repeat the process for 6,314 – 3,133.

Lesson 13: Use place value understanding to decompose to smaller units once using the standard subtraction algorithm, and apply the algorithm to solve word problems using tape diagrams.
Date: 6/28/13

1.E.5

Problem 2

Regroup 1 thousand into 10 hundreds using the subtraction algorithm.

- **T:** (Write 23,422 – 11,510 vertically on the board.)
- **T:** With your partner, read this problem and draw a tape diagram. Label the whole, the known part, and use *B* for the missing part.
- **T:** Record the problem on your board.
- **T:** Look across the numbers. Are we ready to subtract?
- **S:** No!
- **T:** Is the number of units in the top number of the ones column greater than or equal to that of the bottom number? (Point to the 2 and the 0.)
- **S:** Yes, 2 is greater than 0.
- **T:** Is the number of units in the top number of the tens column greater than or equal to that of the bottom number?
- **S:** Yes, 2 is greater than 1.
- **T:** Is the number of units in the top number of the hundreds column greater than or equal to that of the bottom number?
- **S:** No, 4 is less than 5.
- **T:** Tell your partner how to make enough hundreds to subtract.
- **S:** I unbundle 1 unit from the thousands to make 10 hundreds. I now have 2 thousands and 14 hundreds. → I change 1 thousand for 10 hundreds. → I rename 34 hundreds as 20 hundreds and 14 hundreds.
- **T:** Watch as I record that. Now your turn.

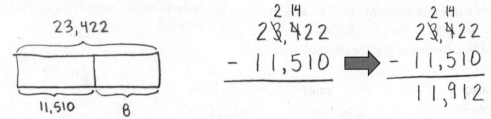

Repeat questioning for the thousands and ten thousands column.

- **T:** Are we ready to subtract?
- **S:** Yes, we're ready to subtract!
- **T:** 2 ones minus 0 ones?
- **S:** 2 ones. (Record 2 in the ones column.)

Continue subtracting across the number from right to left always naming the units.

- **T:** Tell your partner what must be added to 11,510 to result in the sum of 23,422?
- **T:** How do we check a subtraction problem?
- **S:** We can add the difference to the part we knew at first to see if the sum we get equals the whole.

	Lesson 13:	Use place value understanding to decompose to smaller units once using the standard subtraction algorithm, and apply the algorithm to solve word problems using tape diagrams.	1.E.6
	Date:	6/28/13	

T: Please add 11,912 and 11,510. What sum do you get?

S: 23,422, so our answer to the subtraction problem is correct.

T: Label your tape diagram as B = 11,912.

Repeat for 29,014 – 7,503.

Problem 3

Solve a subtraction application problem, regrouping 1 ten thousand into 10 thousands.

The paper mill produced 73,658 boxes of paper. 8,052 boxes have been sold. How many boxes remain?

T: Draw a tape diagram to represent the boxes of paper produced and sold. I'll use the letter P to represent the paper. Record the subtraction problem. Check to see you lined up all units.

T: Am I ready to subtract?

S: No!

T: Work with your partner, asking if the top unit is greater than or equal to the bottom unit. Regroup when needed. Then ask, "Am I ready to subtract?" before you begin subtracting. (Students work.)

S: 73,658 – 8,052 = 65,606.

T: The value of P is 65,606. Tell your partner how many boxes remain in a complete sentence. (65,606 boxes remain.)

T: To check and see if your answer is correct, add the two values of the bar, 8,052 and your answer of 65,606 to see if the sum is the value of the bar, 73,658.

S: (Students add to find their sum matches the value of the bar.)

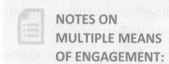

NOTES ON
MULTIPLE MEANS
OF ENGAGEMENT:

Ask students to look at the numbers in the subtraction problem and to think about how the numbers are related. Ask them how they might use their discovery to check to see if their answer is correct. Use the tape diagram to show if 8,052 was subtracted from 73,658 to find the unknown part of the tape diagram, the value of the unknown, 65,606, can be added to the known part of the tape diagram, 8,052. If the sum is the value of the whole tape diagram, the answer is correct.

Repeat with: The library has 50,819 books. 4,506 are checked out. How many books remain in the library?

Lesson 13: Use place value understanding to decompose to smaller units once using the standard subtraction algorithm, and apply the algorithm to solve word problems using tape diagrams.

Date: 6/28/13

1.E.7

© 2013 Common Core, Inc. All rights reserved. commoncore.org

Problem Set (10 minutes)

Students should do their personal best to complete the Problem Set within the allotted 10 minutes. For some classes, it may be appropriate to modify the assignment by specifying which problems they work on first. Some problems do not specify a method for solving. Students solve these problems using the RDW approach used for Application Problems.

Student Debrief (8 minutes)

Lesson Objective: Use place value understanding to decompose to smaller units once using the standard subtraction algorithm, and apply the algorithm to solve word problems using tape diagrams.

The Student Debrief is intended to invite reflection and active processing of the total lesson experience.

Invite students to review their solutions for the Problem Set. They should check work by comparing answers with a partner before going over answers as a class. Look for misconceptions or misunderstandings that can be addressed in the Debrief. Guide students in a conversation to debrief the Problem Set and process the lesson. You may choose to use any combination of the questions below to lead the discussion.

- Compare your answers for Problem 1(a) and 1(b). How is your answer the same, when the problem was different?

- Why do the days and months matter when solving Problem 3?

- Compare Problems 1(a) and 1(f). Does having a larger whole in 1(a) give an answer greater to or less than 1(f)?

- In Problem 4, you used subtraction. But I can say, "I can add 52,411 to 15,614 to result in the sum of 68,025." How can we add and subtract using the same problem?

- Why do we ask, "Are we ready to subtract?"

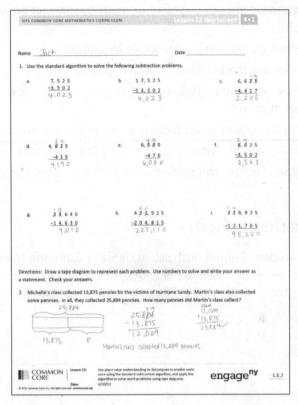

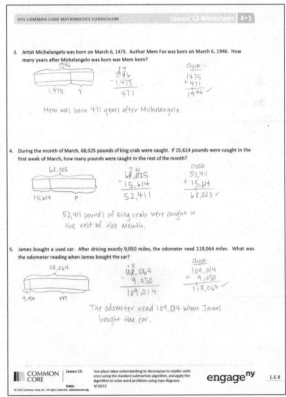

Lesson 13: Use place value understanding to decompose to smaller units once using the standard subtraction algorithm, and apply the algorithm to solve word problems using tape diagrams.
Date: 6/28/13

1.E.8

- When we get our top number ready to subtract do we have to then subtract in order from right to left?

- When do we need to unbundle to subtract?

- What are the benefits to modeling subtraction using number disks?

- Why must the units line up when subtracting? How might our answer change if the numbers were not aligned?

- What happens when there is a zero in the top number of a subtraction problem?

- What happens when there is a zero in the bottom number of a subtraction problem?

- When you are completing word problems, how can you tell that you need to subtract?

Exit Ticket (3 minutes)

After the Student Debrief, instruct students to complete the Exit Ticket. A review of their work will help you assess the students' understanding of the concepts that were presented in the lesson today and plan more effectively for future lessons. You may read the questions aloud to the students.

Lesson 13: Use place value understanding to decompose to smaller units once using the standard subtraction algorithm, and apply the algorithm to solve word problems using tape diagrams.

Date: 6/28/13

© 2013 Common Core, Inc. All rights reserved. **commoncore.org**

1.E.9

Name _____   Date _____

1. Use the standard algorithm to solve the following subtraction problems.

a.   7, 5 2 5
      – 3, 5 0 2

b.   1 7, 5 2 5
       – 1 3, 5 0 2

c.   6, 6 2 5
      – 4, 4 1 7

d.   4, 6 2 5
        – 4 3 5

e.   6, 5 0 0
        – 4 7 0

f.   6, 0 2 5
      – 3, 5 0 2

g.   2 3, 6 4 0
      – 1 4, 6 3 0

h.   4 3 1, 9 2 5
      – 2 0 4, 8 1 5

i.   2 1 9, 9 2 5
      – 1 2 1, 7 0 5

Directions: Draw a tape diagram to represent each problem. Use numbers to solve and write your answer as a statement. Check your answers.

2. What number must be added to 13,875 to result in a sum of 25,884?

COMMON CORE

Lesson 13:   Use place value understanding to decompose to smaller units
             once using the standard subtraction algorithm, and apply the
             algorithm to solve word problems using tape diagrams.
Date: 6/28/13

1.E.10

3. Artist Michelangelo was born on March 6, 1475. Author Mem Fox was born on March 6, 1946. How many years after Michelangelo was born was Mem born?

4. During the month of March, 68,025 pounds of king crab were caught. If 15,614 pounds were caught in the first week of March, how many pounds were caught in the rest of the month?

5. James bought a used car. After driving exactly 9,050 miles, the odometer read 118,064 miles. What was the odometer reading when James bought the car?

Lesson 13:   Use place value understanding to decompose to smaller units
              once using the standard subtraction algorithm, and apply the
              algorithm to solve word problems using tape diagrams.
Date: 6/28/13

1.E.11

Name _____   Date _____

1. a.   8,512   b.   18,042   c.   8,052
        − 2,501   − 4,122   − 1,561

2. Draw a tape diagram to represent the following problem. Use numbers to solve and write your answer as a statement.

    a. What number must be added to 1,575 to result in a sum of 8,625?

Name _____   Date _____

1. Use the standard algorithm to solve the following subtraction problems.

a. 2,431
    − 341

b. 422,431
    − 14,321

c. 422,431
    − 92,420

d. 422,431
   − 392,420

e. 982,430
    − 92,300

f. 243,089
    − 137,079

g. 2,431 − 920 =

h. 892,431 − 520,800 =

2. What number must be added to 14,056 to result in a sum of 32,713?

COMMON CORE™ | **Lesson 13:** Use place value understanding to decompose to smaller units once using the standard subtraction algorithm, and apply the algorithm to solve word problems using tape diagrams.

Date: 6/28/13 | 1.E.13

Directions: Draw a tape diagram to model each problem. Use numbers to solve and write your answers as a statement. Check your answers.

3.   An elementary school collected 1,705 bottles for a recycling program. A high school also collected some bottles. Both schools collected 3,627 bottles combined. How many bottles did the high school collect?

4.   A computer shop sold $356,291 worth of computers and accessories. It sold $43,720 worth of accessories. How much did the computer shop sell in computers?

5.   The population of a city is 538,381. In that population, 148,170 are children.
   a.   How many adults live in the city?

   b.   186,101 of the adults are males. How many adults are female?

Use place value understanding to decompose to smaller units
          once using the standard subtraction algorithm, and apply the
          algorithm to solve word problems using tape diagrams.   **1.E.14**
Date: 6/28/13

Lesson 14

Objective: Use place value understanding to decompose to smaller units up to 3 times using the standard subtraction algorithm, and apply the algorithm to solve word problems using tape diagrams.

Suggested Lesson Structure

■ Fluency Practice   (10 minutes)
■ Application Problem   (6 minutes)
■ Concept Development   (35 minutes)
■ Student Debrief   (9 minutes)
   Total Time   **(60 minutes)**

Fluency Practice (10 minutes)

- Base Ten Thousand Units **4.NBT.2**   (2 minutes)
- Find the Difference **4.NBT.4**   (4 minutes)
- Convert Units **4.MD.1**   (4 minutes)

Base Ten Thousand Units (2 minutes)

Materials: (S) Personal white boards, place value chart to ten thousands

Note: Reviewing this fluency will help students work towards mastery of understanding base ten units.

   T: (Project 8 ten thousands = _____.) Write the number in standard form.
   S: 80,000.

Continue with the following possible sequence: 9 ten thousands, 10 ten thousands, 13 ten thousands, 19 ten thousands, 20 ten thousands, 30 ten thousands, 70 ten thousands, 700 ten thousands, 715 ten thousands, 347 ten thousands.

Lesson 14:   Use place value understanding to decompose to smaller units
up to 3 times using the standard subtraction algorithm, and
apply the algorithm to solve word problems using tape diagrams.
Date: 6/28/13

Find the Difference (4 minutes)

Materials: (S) Personal white boards

Note: Reviewing this mental math fluency will prepare students for understanding the importance of the subtraction algorithm.

  T: (Write 735 – 203 =_____.) Write a subtraction sentence horizontally or vertically.
  S: (Students write 735 – 203 = 532.)

Repeat process and sequence for 7,045 – 4,003; 845 – 18; 5,725 – 915; and 34,736 – 2,806.

Convert Units (4 minutes)

Note: Reviewing these unit conversions that were learned in third grade will help prepare the students to solve problems with metric measurement and its relationship to place value in Module 2.

  T: (Write 1 m = ___ cm.) How many centimeters are in a meter?
  S: 1 m = 100 cm.

Repeat process for 2 m, 3 m, 8 m, 8 m 50 cm, 7 m 50 cm, and 4 m 25 cm.

  T: (Write 100 cm = ___ m.) Say the answer.
  S: 100 m = 1 m.
  T: (Write 150 cm = ___ m ___ cm.) Say the answer.
  S: 150 cm = 1 m 50 cm.

Repeat process for 250 cm, 350 cm, 950 cm, and 725 cm.

Application Problem (6 minutes)

In one year, the animal shelter bought 25,460 pounds of dog food. That amount was 10 times the amount of cat food purchased in the month of July. How much cat food was purchased in July?

Bonus: If the cats ate 1,462 pounds of the cat food, how much cat food was left?

25,460 is 10 times as many as 2,546.

2,546 pounds of cat food was purchased in the month of July.

Bonus:
$$\begin{array}{r} 2,\overset{4}{\overset{\ }{5}}\overset{14}{\overset{\ }{4}}6 \\ -\ 1,462 \\ \hline 1,084 \end{array}$$

1,084 pounds of cat food was left.

Note: This application problem incorporates prior knowledge of 10 times as many with the objective of decomposing to smaller units in order to subtract.

COMMON CORE™

Lesson 14:   Use place value understanding to decompose to smaller units
             up to 3 times using the standard subtraction algorithm, and
             apply the algorithm to solve word problems using tape diagrams.
Date: 6/28/13

1.E.16

© 2013 Common Core, Inc. All rights reserved. commoncore.org

Concept Development (35 minutes)

Materials: (T) Place value chart (S) Personal white boards

Problem 1

Subtract, decomposing twice.

T: (Write 22,397 – 3,745 vertically on the board.)

T: Let's read this subtraction problem together. Watch as I draw a tape diagram labeling the whole, the known part and the unknown part using a variable. Now, your turn.

T: Record the problem on your board.

T: Look across the digits. Am I ready to subtract?

S: No!

T: We look across the top number to see if I have enough units in each column. Is the number of units in the top number of the ones column greater than or equal to that of the bottom number?

S: Yes, 7 ones is greater than 5 ones.

T: Is the number of units in the top number of the tens column greater than or equal to that of the bottom number?

S: Yes, 9 tens is greater than 4 tens.

T: Is the number of units in the top number of the hundreds column greater than or equal to that of the bottom number?

S: No, 3 hundreds is less than 7 hundreds. We can unbundle 1 thousand as 10 hundreds to make 1 thousand and 13 hundreds. I can subtract the hundreds column now.

T: Watch as I record that. Now, it's your turn to record the change.

T: Is the number of units in the top number of the thousands column greater than or equal to that of the bottom number?

S: No, 1 thousand is less than 3 thousands. We can unbundle 1 ten thousand to 10 thousands to make 1 ten thousand and 11 thousands. I can subtract in the thousands column now.

T: Watch as I record. Now, it's your turn to record the change.

T: Is the number of units in the top number of the ten thousands column greater than or equal to that of the bottom number?

S: Yes.

T: Are we ready to subtract?

S: Yes, we're ready to subtract!

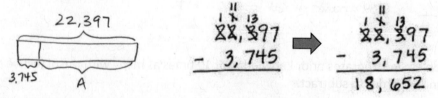

Lesson 14: Use place value understanding to decompose to smaller units up to 3 times using the standard subtraction algorithm, and apply the algorithm to solve word problems using tape diagrams.

Date: 6/28/13

1.E.17

© 2013 Common Core, Inc. All rights reserved. commoncore.org

T: 7 ones minus 5 ones?

S: 2 ones. (Record 2 in the ones column.)

Continue subtracting across the problem always naming the units.

T: Say the complete equation with me.

S: 22,397 minus 3,745 equals 18,652.

T: Check your answer using addition.

S: Our answer is correct because 18,652 plus 3,745 = 22,397.

T: What is the value of *A* in the tape diagram?

S: A equals 18,652.

Problem 2

Subtract: 210,290 – 45,720, decomposing three times.

T: (Write 210,290 – 45,720 vertically on the board.)

T: With your partner, draw a tape diagram to represent the whole, the known part, and the missing part.

T: Record the subtraction problem on your board.

T: Look across the numbers. Are we ready to subtract?

S: No!

T: Look across the top number's digits to see if we have enough units in each column. Is the number of units in the top number of the ones column greater than or equal to that of the bottom number? (Point to the zeros in the ones column.)

S: Yes, 0 equals 0.

T: We are ready to subtract in the ones column. Is the number of units in the top number of the tens column greater than or equal to that of the bottom number?

S: Yes, 9 is greater than 2.

MP.5 T: We are ready to subtract in the tens column. Is the number of units in the top number of the hundreds column greater than or equal to that of the bottom number?

S: No, 2 hundreds is less than 7 hundreds.

T: There are no thousands to unbundle so we look to the ten thousands. We can unbundle 1 ten thousand to 10 thousands. Unbundle 10 thousands to make 9 thousands and 12 hundreds. Now we can subtract the hundreds column.

Repeat questioning for the thousands, ten thousands, and hundred thousands place, recording the renaming of units in the algorithm.

T: Are we ready to subtract?

S: Yes, we're ready to subtract!

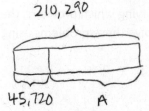

| Lesson 14: | Use place value understanding to decompose to smaller units up to 3 times using the standard subtraction algorithm, and apply the algorithm to solve word problems using tape diagrams. | **1.E.18** |
| Date: | 6/28/13 | |

© 2013 Common Core, Inc. All rights reserved. **commoncore.org**

T: 0 ones minus 0 ones?

S: 0 ones.

T: 9 tens minus 2 tens?

S: 7 tens.

Have partners continuing subtracting across the algorithm right to left always naming the units.

T: Read the entire equation to your partner and complete your tape diagram by labeling the variable.

S: The difference between 210,290 and 45,720 is 164,570.

Problem 3

Use the subtraction algorithm to solve a word problem, modeled with a tape diagram, decomposing units 3 times.

Bryce needed to purchase a large order of computer supplies for his company. He was allowed to spend $859,239 on computers. However, he ended up only spending $272,650. How much money did Bryce have left?

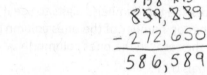
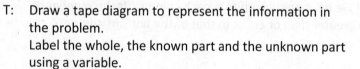

T: Read the problem with me. Tell your partner the information we know.

S: We know he can spend $859,239. And we know he only spent $272,650.

T: Draw a tape diagram to represent the information in the problem.
Label the whole, the known part and the unknown part using a variable.

T: Tell me the problem we must solve and write it on your board.

S: $859,239 – $272,650.

T: Work with your partner, asking if the top unit is greater than or equal to that of the bottom unit. Regroup when needed. Then ask, "Are we ready to subtract?" before you begin subtracting.

S: (Students solve.)

S: $859,239 – $272,650 = $586,589.

T: Say your answer as a statement.

S: Bryce has $586,589 left.

Problem Set (10 minutes)

Students should do their personal best to complete the Problem Set within the allotted 10 minutes. For some classes, it may be appropriate to modify the assignment by specifying which problems they work on first. Some problems do not specify a method for solving. Students solve these problems using the RDW approach used for Application Problems.

COMMON CORE™

Lesson 14: Use place value understanding to decompose to smaller units up to 3 times using the standard subtraction algorithm, and apply the algorithm to solve word problems using tape diagrams.

Date: 6/28/13

1.E.19

© 2013 Common Core, Inc. All rights reserved. commoncore.org

Student Debrief (9 minutes)

Lesson Objective: Use place value understanding to decompose to smaller units up to 3 times using the standard subtraction algorithm, and apply the algorithm to solve word problems using tape diagrams.

The Student Debrief is intended to invite reflection and active processing of the total lesson experience.

Invite students to review their solutions for the Problem Set. They should check work by comparing answers with a partner before going over answers as a class. Look for misconceptions or misunderstandings that can be addressed in the Debrief. Guide students in a conversation to debrief the Problem Set and process the lesson. You may choose to use any combination of the questions below to lead the discussion.

- What pattern did you notice between Problems 1(a) and 1(b)?

- How was setting up the problem to complete Problem 4 different from setting up the other problems? What did you need to be sure to do? Why?

- Explain to your partner how to solve Problem 1(e). How can you make more ones when there aren't any tens from which to regroup?

- How is the complexity of this lesson different from the complexity of yesterday's lesson?

- In which column can you begin subtracting, when you are ready to subtract? (Any column.)

- You are using a variable, or a letter, to represent the unknown in each tape diagram. Tell your partner how you determine what variable to use and how it helps you to solve the problem.

- Our tape diagram shows us we are looking for a missing part when subtracting. After subtracting, if we add the two parts together, what should the sum be?

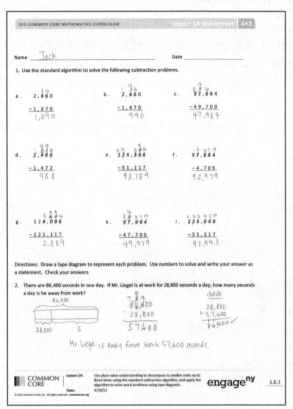

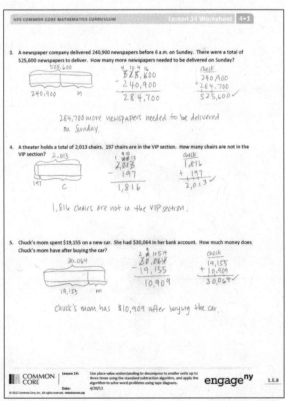

Lesson 14:   Use place value understanding to decompose to smaller units up to 3 times using the standard subtraction algorithm, and apply the algorithm to solve word problems using tape diagrams.
Date: 6/28/13

1.E.20

Exit Ticket (3 minutes)

After the Student Debrief, instruct students to complete the Exit Ticket. A review of their work will help you assess the students' understanding of the concepts that were presented in the lesson today and plan more effectively for future lessons. You may read the questions aloud to the students.

COMMON CORE™

Lesson 14:   Use place value understanding to decompose to smaller units
up to 3 times using the standard subtraction algorithm, and
apply the algorithm to solve word problems using tape diagrams.

Date: 6/28/13

1.E.21

Name _____   Date _____

1. Use the standard algorithm to solve the following subtraction problems.

a.   2,460
    −1,370

b.   2,460
    −1,470

c.   97,684
    −49,700

d.   2,460
    −1,472

e.   124,306
   −31,117

f.   97,684
    −4,705

g.   124,006
   −121,117

h.   97,684
    −47,705

i.   124,060
   −31,117

Directions: Draw a tape diagram to represent each problem. Use numbers to solve and write your answer as a statement. Check your answers.

2. There are 86,400 seconds in one day. If Mr. Liegel is at work for 28,800 seconds a day, how many seconds a day is he away from work?

Lesson 14:   Use place value understanding to decompose to smaller units up to 3 times using the standard subtraction algorithm, and apply the algorithm to solve word problems using tape diagrams.

Date: 6/28/13

1.E.22

3. A newspaper company delivered 240,900 newspapers before 6 a.m. on Sunday. There were a total of 525,600 newspapers to deliver. How many more newspapers needed to be delivered on Sunday?

4. A theater holds a total of 2,013 chairs. 197 chairs are in the VIP section. How many chairs are not in the VIP section?

5. Chuck's mom spent $19,155 on a new car. She had $30,064 in her bank account. How much money does Chuck's mom have after buying the car?

Lesson 14:

Date: 6/28/13

Use place value understanding to decompose to smaller units up to 3 times using the standard subtraction algorithm, and apply the algorithm to solve word problems using tape diagrams.

1.E.23

Name _____   Date _____

Directions: Use the standard algorithm to solve the following subtraction problems.

1.
            1 9, 3 5 0
        −   5, 7 6 1

2.   32,010 − 2,546

Directions: Draw a tape diagram to represent the following problem. Use numbers to solve and write your answer as a statement. Check your answer.

3. A doughnut shop sold 1,232 doughnuts in one day. If they sold 876 doughnuts in the morning, how many doughnuts were sold during the rest of the day?

COMMON CORE™

Lesson 14:   Use place value understanding to decompose to smaller units
up to 3 times using the standard subtraction algorithm, and
apply the algorithm to solve word problems using tape diagrams.
Date: 6/28/13

1.E.24

Name _____   Date _____

1. Use the standard algorithm to solve the following subtraction problems.

a.
```
   71,989
 - 21,492
```

b.
```
  371,989
 - 96,492
```

c.
```
  371,089
 - 25,192
```

d.
```
  879,989
 -721,492
```

e.
```
  879,009
 -788,492
```

f.
```
  879,989
 - 21,070
```

g.
```
  879,000
 - 21,989
```

h.
```
  279,389
 -191,492
```

i.
```
  500,989
 -242,000
```

COMMON CORE | Lesson 14:   Use place value understanding to decompose to smaller units
up to 3 times using the standard subtraction algorithm, and
apply the algorithm to solve word problems using tape diagrams.

Date: 6/28/13

© 2013 Common Core, Inc. All rights reserved. commoncore.org

1.E.2

Directions: Draw a tape diagram to represent each problem. Use numbers to solve and write your answer as a statement.

2. Jason ordered 239,021 pounds of flour to be used in his 25 bakeries. The company delivering the flour showed up with 451,202 pounds. How many extra pounds of flour were delivered?

3. In May, the New York Public Library had 124,061 books checked out. Of those books, 31,117 were mystery books. How many of checked out books were not mystery books?

4. A Class A dump truck can haul 239,000 pounds of dirt. A Class C dump truck can haul 600,200 pounds of dirt. How many more pounds can a Class C truck haul than a Class A truck?

Lesson 14: Use place value understanding to decompose to smaller units
up to 3 times using the standard subtraction algorithm, and
apply the algorithm to solve word problems using tape diagrams.

Date: 6/28/13

Lesson 15

Objective: Use place value understanding to fluently decompose to smaller units multiple times in any place using the standard subtraction algorithm, and apply the algorithm to solve word problems using tape diagrams.

Suggested Lesson Structure

■ Fluency Practice	(11 minutes)	
■ Application Problem	(6 minutes)	
■ Concept Development	(32 minutes)	
■ Student Debrief	(11 minutes)	
Total Time	**(60 minutes)**	

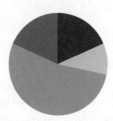

Fluency Practice (11 minutes)

- Place Value **4.NBT.2**   (3 minutes)
- Find the Difference **4.NBT.4**   (4 minutes)
- Convert Units **4.MD.1**   (4 minutes)

Place Value (3 minutes)

Note: Practicing these skills in isolation will help lay a foundation for conceptually understanding this lesson's content.

T: (Write 4,598.) Say the number.

S: 4,598.

T: What digit is in the tens place?

S: 9.

T: (Underline 9.) What's the value of the 9?

S: 90.

T: State the value of the digit 4.

S: 4,000.

T: 5?

S: 500.

Repeat using the following possible sequence: 69,708; 398,504; and 8,253,967.

Find the Difference (4 minutes)

Lesson 15:	Use place value understanding to fluently decompose to smaller units multiple times in any place using the standard subtraction algorithm, and apply the algorithm to solve word problems using tape diagrams.	
Date:	6/28/13	

Materials: (S) Personal white boards

Note: Reviewing this mental math fluency will prepare students for understanding the importance of the subtraction algorithm.

    T: (Write 846 – 304 = _____.) Write a subtraction sentence horizontally or vertically.

    S: (Students write 846 – 304 = 542.)

Repeat process and sequence for 8,056 – 5,004; 935 – 17; 4,625 – 815; and 45,836 – 2,906.

Convert Units (4 minutes)

Note: Reviewing these unit conversions that were learned in Grade 3 will help prepare the students to solve problems with meters and centimeters in Module 2, Topic A.

Materials: (S) Personal white boards

    T: Count by 20 centimeters. When you get to 100 centimeters, say 1 meter.

    S: 20cm, 40 cm, 60 cm, 80 cm, 1 m, 120 cm, 140 cm, 160 cm, 180 cm, 2 m.

Repeat process, this time pulling out the meter (e.g., 1 m 20 cm, 1 m 40 cm, etc.).

    T: (Write 130 cm = ___ m ___ cm.) On your boards, fill in the blanks.

    S: (Students compose 130 centimeters into 1 meter 30 centimeters.)

Repeat process for 103 cm, 175 cm, 345 cm, and 708 cm for composing to meters.

Application Problem (6 minutes)

When the amusement park opened, the number on the counter at the gate read 928,614. At the end of the day, the counter read 931,682. How many people went through the gate that day?

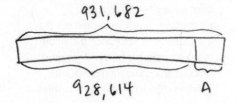

$$\begin{array}{r} 2\ \overset{11}{1}\quad\overset{7}{8}\ \overset{12}{2} \\ 9\,8\,1,\,6\,8\,2 \\ -\,9\,2\,8,\,6\,1\,4 \\ \hline 3,\,0\,6\,8 \end{array}$$

3,068 people went through the gate that day.

Note: At times we ask students to use a specific strategy and at other times we see what they do independently. In the spirit of **MP.5**, this question sees what tools they choose independently.

COMMON CORE™   Lesson 15:   Use place value understanding to fluently decompose to smaller units
                                     multiple times in any place using the standard subtraction algorithm,   1.E.28
                        Date: and apply the algorithm to solve word problems using tape diagrams.
                                     6/28/13

© 2013 Common Core, Inc. All rights reserved. **commoncore.org**

Concept Development (32 minutes)

Materials: (S) Personal white boards , place value charts

Problem 1

Regroup units 5 times to subtract.

Write 253,421 – 75,832 vertically on the board.

T: Say this problem with me.

T: Work with your partner to draw a tape diagram representing this problem.

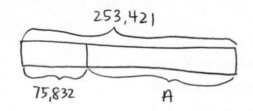

T: What is the whole amount?

S: 253,421.

T: What part are we separating out?

S: 75,832.

T: Look across the top number, 253,421, to see if we have
enough units in each column to subtract 75,832.
Are we ready to subtract?

S: No!

T: Is the number of units in the top number of the ones
column greater than or equal to that of the bottom
number? (Point to the 1 and 2 in the equation.)

S: No, 1 one is less than 2 ones.

T: What should we do?

S: Change 1 ten for 10 ones. That means you have 1 ten
and 11 ones.

T: Is the number of units in the top number of the tens
column greater than or equal to that of the bottom
number? (Point to tens column.)

S: No, 1 ten is less than 3 tens.

T: What should we do?

S: Change 1 hundred for 10 tens. You have 3 hundreds and 11 tens.

T: The tens column is ready to subtract.

Have partners continue questioning if the top number is greater than or equal to the bottom unit across all

> **NOTES ON
> MULTIPLE MEANS OF
> ENGAGEMENT:**
>
> Students of all abilities will benefit
> from using addition to check
> subtraction. Students should see that
> if the sum does not match the whole
> their calculation is faulty. They must
> subtract again and then check with
> addition. Challenge students to think
> about how they use this check strategy
> in everyday life. We do this all of the
> time when we add-up to another
> number.

**COMMON
CORE™** | **Lesson 15:** Use place value understanding to fluently decompose to smaller units
multiple times in any place using the standard subtraction algorithm,
and apply the algorithm to solve word problems using tape diagrams.   **1.E.29**
| Date: 6/28/13

units, regrouping where needed.

T: Are we ready to subtract?

S: Yes, we're ready to subtract!

T: Go ahead and subtract.

S: (Students do so.)

T: State the difference to your partner. Label the missing part in your tape diagram.

S: The difference between 253,421 and 75,832 is 177,589.

T: Add the difference with the part you knew to see if your answer is correct.

S: It is. The sum of the parts is 253,421.

Problem 2

Decompose numbers from 1 thousand and 1 million into smaller units to subtract, modeled with number disks.

Write 1,000 – 528 vertically on the board.

T: With your partner, read this problem and draw a tape diagram. Label what you know and the unknown.

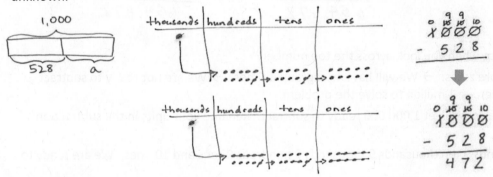

T: Record the problem on your board.

T: Look across the units in the top number. Are we ready to subtract?

S: No!

T: Is the number of units in the top number of the ones column greater than or equal to that of the bottom number? (Point to 0 and 8 in the ones column.)

S: No. 0 ones is less than 8 ones.

T: I need to ungroup 1 unit from the tens. What do you notice?

S: There are no tens to ungroup.

T: We can look to the hundreds. (There are no hundreds to ungroup either.)

T: In order to get 10 ones, we need to regroup 1 thousand.

> **NOTES ON MULTIPLE MEANS OF ACTION AND EXPRESSION:**
>
> Encourage students who notice a pattern of repeated nines when subtracting across multiple zeros to express this pattern in writing. Allow students to identify why this happens using manipulatives and/or in writing. Allow students to slowly transition into recording this particular unbundling across zeros as nines as they become fluent with using the algorithm.

MP.6

COMMON CORE

Lesson 15: Use place value understanding to fluently decompose to smaller units multiple times in any place using the standard subtraction algorithm, and apply the algorithm to solve word problems using tape diagrams.

Date: 6/28/13

1.E.30

Watch as I represent the ungrouping in my subtraction problem. (Model using the disks and rename units in the problem simultaneously.) Now your turn.

T: Am I ready to subtract?

S: Yes, we're ready to subtract!

T: Solve for 9 hundreds 9 tens 10 ones minus 5 hundreds 2 tens 8 ones.

S: 1,000 – 528 is 472.

T: Can you check?

S: The sum of 472 and 528 is 1000.

T: (Write 1,000,000 – 345,528 vertically on the board.)

T: Read this problem and draw a tape diagram to represent the subtraction problem.

T: Record the subtraction problem on your board.

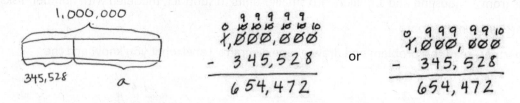

T: What do you notice when you look across the top number?

S: There are a lot more zeros. → We will have to regroup 6 times. → We are not ready to subtract. We will have to regroup 1 million to solve the problem.

T: Work with your partner to get 1,000,000 ready to subtract. Rename your units in the subtraction problem.

S: 9 hundred thousands 9 ten thousands 9 thousands 9 hundreds 9 tens and 10 ones. We are ready to subtract!

S: 1,000,000 minus 345,528 equals 654,472.

T: To check your answer, add the parts to see if you get the correct whole amount.

S: We did! We got one million when we added the parts.

Problem 3

Solve a word problem decomposing units multiple times.

Last year, there were 620,073 people in attendance at a local parade. This year, there were 456,795 people in attendance. How many more people were in attendance last year?

T: Read with me.

T: Represent this information in a tape diagram.

T: Work with your partner to write a subtraction problem using the information in the tape diagram.

T: Look across the top number to see if the units in the top number are greater than or equal to that of the bottom number. Are you ready to subtract?

Lesson 15:

Date:

Use place value understanding to fluently decompose to smaller units multiple times in any place using the standard subtraction algorithm, and apply the algorithm to solve word problems using tape diagrams.

6/28/13

1.E.31

S: No, I do not have enough ones in the top number. I need to unbundle 1 ten to make 10 ones. Then I have 6 tens and 13 ones.

T: Continue to check if you are ready to subtract in each column. When you are ready to subtract, solve.

S: 620,073 minus 456,795 equals 163,278. There were 163,278 more people in attendance last year.

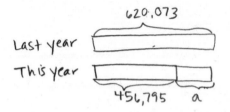 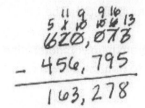

Problem Set (10 minutes)

Students should do their personal best to complete the Problem Set within the allotted 10 minutes. For some classes, it may be appropriate to modify the assignment by specifying which problems they work on first. Some problems do not specify a method for solving. Students solve these problems using the RDW approach used for Application Problems.

Student Debrief (11 minutes)

Lesson Objective: Use place value understanding to fluently decompose to smaller units multiple times in any place using the standard subtraction algorithm, and apply the algorithm to solve word problems using tape diagrams.

The Student Debrief is intended to invite reflection and active processing of the total lesson experience.

Invite students to review their solutions for the Problem Set. They should check work by comparing answers with a partner before going over answers as a class. Look for misconceptions or misunderstandings that can be addressed in the Debrief. Guide students in a conversation to debrief the Problem Set and process the lesson. You may choose to use any combination of the questions below to lead the discussion.

- Problem 1(e) and 1(f) were similar. Did anyone notice a pattern that could be used to solve this problem?

- How did your tape diagrams differ in Problems 2, 3, and 4?

- How do you know when you are ready to subtract across the algorithm?

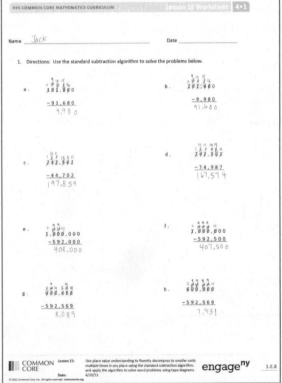

Lesson 15:

Date:

Use place value understanding to fluently decompose to smaller units multiple times in any place using the standard subtraction algorithm, and apply the algorithm to solve word problems using tape diagrams.

6/28/13

1.E.32

- How can you check your answer when subtracting?
- Is there a number that you can subtract from 1,000,000 without decomposing across to the ones (other than 1,000,000)? 100,000? 10,000?
- How can decomposing multiple times be challenging?
- How does the tape diagram help you determine which operation to use to find the answer?

Exit Ticket (3 minutes)

After the Student Debrief, instruct students to complete the Exit Ticket. A review of their work will help you assess the students' understanding of the concepts that were presented in the lesson today and plan more effectively for future lessons. You may read the questions aloud to the students.

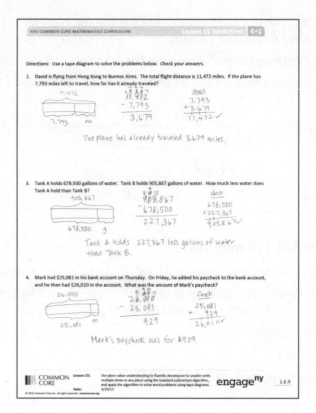

Lesson 15:

Date:

Use place value understanding to fluently decompose to smaller units multiple times in any place using the standard subtraction algorithm, and apply the algorithm to solve word problems using tape diagrams.

6/28/13

1.E.33

Name _____   Date _____

1. Directions: Use the standard subtraction algorithm to solve the problems below.

a..   1 0 1 , 6 6 0

        – 9 1 , 6 8 0

b.   1 0 1 , 6 6 0

        – 9 , 9 8 0

c.   2 4 2 , 5 6 1

        – 4 4 , 7 0 2

d.   2 4 2 , 5 6 1

        – 7 4 , 9 8 7

e.   1 , 0 0 0 , 0 0 0

        – 5 9 2 , 0 0 0

f.   1 , 0 0 0 , 0 0 0

        – 5 9 2 , 5 0 0

g.   6 0 0 , 6 5 8

        – 5 9 2 , 5 6 9

h.   6 0 0 , 0 0 0

        – 5 9 2 , 5 6 9

Lesson 15:   Use place value understanding to fluently decompose to smaller units
                   multiple times in any place using the standard subtraction algorithm,
                   and apply the algorithm to solve word problems using tape diagrams.

Date: 6/28/13

Directions: Use a tape diagram to solve the problems below. Check your answers.

2. David is flying from Hong Kong to Buenos Aires. The total flight distance is 11,472 miles. If the plane has 7,793 miles left to travel, how far has it already traveled?

3. Tank A holds 678,500 gallons of water. Tank B holds 905,867 gallons of water. How much less water does Tank A hold than Tank B?

4. Mark had $25,081 in his bank account on Thursday. On Friday, he added his paycheck to the bank account, and he then had $26,010 in the account. What was the amount of Mark's paycheck?

COMMON CORE™ Lesson 15:   Use place value understanding to fluently decompose to smaller units multiple times in any place using the standard subtraction algorithm, and apply the algorithm to solve word problems using tape diagrams.

Date: 6/28/13

1.E.35

Name _____   Date _____

Directions: Draw a tape diagram to model each problem and solve.

1. 956,204 – 780,169 =_____

2. A construction company was building a stone wall on Main Street. 100,000 stones were delivered to the site. On Monday they used 15,631 stones. How many stones remain for the rest of the week? Write your answer as a statement.

COMMON CORE™ | **Lesson 15:**   Use place value understanding to fluently decompose to smaller units multiple times in any place using the standard subtraction algorithm, and apply the algorithm to solve word problems using tape diagrams.   **1.E.36**

Date: 6/28/13

Name _____   Date _____

1 . Directions: Use the standard subtraction algorithm to solve the problems below.

a .
```
    9 , 6 5 6
  -   8 3 8
```

b .
```
   5 9 , 6 5 6
  -  5 , 8 8 0
```

c .
```
  7 5 9 , 6 5 6
 - 5 7 9 , 9 8 9
```

d .
```
  2 9 4 , 1 5 0
 - 1 6 6 , 3 7 0
```

e .
```
  2 9 4 , 1 5 0
 - 2 3 9 , 0 8 9
```

f .
```
  2 9 4 , 1 5 0
 -   9 6 , 4 0 0
```

g .
```
  8 0 0 , 5 0 0
 -   7 9 , 9 8 9
```

h .
```
  8 0 0 , 5 0 0
 -   4 5 , 5 0 0
```

i .
```
  8 0 0 , 5 0 0
 - 2 7 6 , 6 6 4
```

COMMON CORE™ | Lesson 15: | Use place value understanding to fluently decompose to smaller units multiple times in any place using the standard subtraction algorithm, and apply the algorithm to solve word problems using tape diagrams.

Date: 6/28/13

1.E.37

Directions: Use a tape diagram to solve the problems below. Check your answers.

2. A fishing boat was out to sea for 6 months and traveled a total of 8,578 miles. In the first month, the boat traveled 659 miles. How many miles did the fishing boat travel during the remaining 5 months?

3.   A national monument had 160,747 visitors during the first week of September. A total of 759,656 people visited the monument in September. How many people visited the monument in September after the first week?

4. Shadow Software Company earned a total of $800,000 selling programs during the year 2012. $125,300 of that amount was used to pay expenses of the company. How much profit did Shadow Software Company make in the year 2012?

5. At the local aquarium, Bubba the Seal ate a 25,634 grams of fish during the week. If, on the first day of the week, he ate 6,987 grams of fish, how many grams of fish did he eat during the remainder of the week?

Lesson 15:

Date:

Use place value understanding to fluently decompose to smaller units multiple times in any place using the standard subtraction algorithm, and apply the algorithm to solve word problems using tape diagrams.

6/28/13

1.E.38

Lesson 16

Objective: Solve two-step word problems using the standard subtraction algorithm fluently modeled with tape diagrams and assess the reasonableness of answers using rounding.

Suggested Lesson Structure

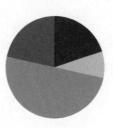

■ Fluency Practice   (12 minutes)
  Application Problem   (5 minutes)
■ Concept Development   (30 minutes)
■ Student Debrief   (13 minutes)
   Total Time   **(60 minutes)**

Fluency Practice (12 minutes)

▪ Convert Meters and Centimeters to Centimeters **4.MD.1**   (8 minutes)
▪ Compare Numbers **4.NBT.2**   (4 minutes)

Sprint: Convert Meters and Centimeters to Centimeters (8 minutes)

Materials: (S) Convert Meters and Centimeters to Centimeters Sprint

Note: Reviewing unit conversions that were learned in Grade 3 will help prepare the students to solve problems with meters and centimeters in Module 2, Topic A.

Compare Numbers (4 minutes)

Materials: (S) Personal white boards

Note: Reviewing this fluency will help students work towards mastery of comparing numbers.

   T: (Project 342,006 _____ 94,983.) On your boards, compare the numbers writing the greater than, less than, or equal symbol.

   S: (Students write 342,006 > 94,893.)

Repeat for possible sequence: 7 thousands 5 hundreds 8 tens _____ 6 ten thousands 5 hundreds 8 ones, and 9 hundred thousands 8 thousands 9 hundreds 3 tens _____ 807,820.

Lesson 16:

Date:

Solve two-step word problems using the standard subtraction algorithm fluently modeled with tape diagrams and assess the reasonableness of answers using rounding.

6/28/13

1.E.39

Application Problem (5 minutes)

For the weekend basketball playoffs, a total of 61,941 tickets were sold. 29,855 tickets were sold for Saturday's games. The rest of the tickets were sold for Sunday's games. How many tickets were sold for Sunday's games?

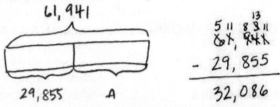

Note: This Application Problem reviews content from the prior lesson of using the subtraction algorithm with multiple regroupings.

Concept Development (30 minutes)

Materials: (S) Personal white boards

Problem 1

Solve a two-step word problem, modeled with a tape diagram, assessing reasonableness of answer using rounding.

A company has 3 locations with 70,010 employees all together. Their first location has 34,857 employees. Their second location has 17,595 employees. How many employees work in their third location?

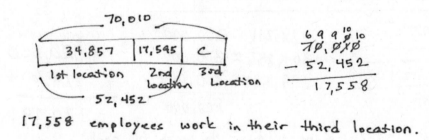

T: Read with me. Take 2 minutes to draw and label a tape diagram.

Circulate and encourage the students: "Can you draw something?" "What can you draw?"

T: (After 2 minutes.) Tell your partner the known and unknown information.

S: We know the total number of employees and the employees at the first and second locations. We don't know how many employees are at the third location.

Lesson 16:   Solve two-step word problems using the standard subtraction
              algorithm fluently modeled with tape diagrams and assess the
              reasonableness of answers using rounding.   1.E.40
Date: 6/28/13

© 2013 Common Core, Inc. All rights reserved. commoncore.org

T: Use your tape diagram to estimate the number of employees at the third location. Explain your reasoning to your partner.

S: I rounded the number of employees. 30,000 + 20,000 = 50,000 and I know that the total number of employees is about 70,000. That means that there would be about 20,000 employees at the third location.

T: Now, find the precise answer. Work with your partner to do so.

Give students time to work.

T: Label the missing part on your diagram and make a statement of the solution.

S: There are 17,558 employees at the third location.

T: Is your answer reasonable?

S: Yes, because 17,558 rounded to the nearest ten thousand is 20,000, and that was our estimate.

> **NOTES ON MULTIPLE MEANS OF ACTION AND EXPRESSION:**
>
> Students working below grade level may not consider whether their answer makes sense. Guide students to choose the sensible operation and check their answers. Encourage students to reread the problem after solving and to ask themselves, "Does my answer make sense?" If not, ask, "What else can I try?"

Problem 2

Solve two-step word problems, modeled with a tape diagram, assessing reasonableness of answer using rounding.

Owen's goal is to have 1 million people visit his new website within the first four months of it being launched. Below is a chart showing the number of visitors each month. How many more visitors does he need in Month 4 to reach his goal?

	Month			
	Month 1	Month 2	Month 3	Month 4
Visitors	228,211	301,856	299,542	

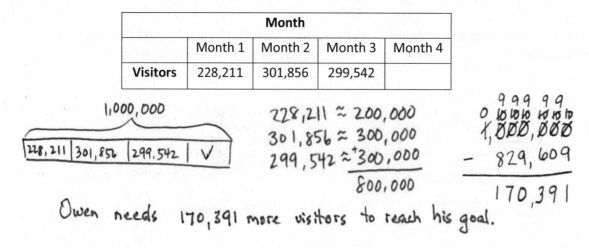

T: With your partner draw a tape diagram. Tell your partner your strategy for solving this problem.

S: We can find the sum of the number of visitors during the first 3 months. Then, we subtract that from 1 million to find how many more visitors are needed to reach his goal.

T: Make an estimate for the number of visitors in Month 4. Explain your reasoning to your partner.

Lesson 16:   Solve two-step word problems using the standard subtraction algorithm fluently modeled with tape diagrams and assess the reasonableness of answers using rounding.

Date: 6/28/13

S: I can round to the nearest hundred thousand and estimate. Owen will need about 200,000 visitors to reach his goal.
    → I rounded to the nearest ten thousand to get a closer estimate of 170,000 visitors.

T: Find the total for the first 3 months. What is the precise sum?

S: 829,609.

T: Compare the actual and estimated solutions. Is your answer reasonable?

S: Yes, because our estimate of 200,000 is near 170,391.
    → Rounded to the nearest hundred thousand 170,391 is 200,000. → 170,391 rounded to the nearest ten thousand is 170,000 which was also our estimate, so our solution is reasonable.

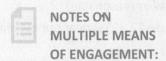

NOTES ON MULTIPLE MEANS OF ENGAGEMENT:

Challenge students working above grade level to expand their thinking and to figure out another way to solve the two-step problem. Is there another strategy that would work?

Problem 3

Solve a two-step word problem with a *compare with smaller unknown* base.

There were 12,345 people at a concert on Saturday night. On Sunday night, there were 1,795 fewer people at the concert than on Saturday night. How many people attended the concert on both nights?

Sat. [12,345]
Sun. [   ]   P

$$12,\cancel{3}45 \quad\quad 12,345$$
$$-\ \ 1,795 \quad\quad +10,550$$
$$\overline{10,550} \quad\quad \overline{22,895}$$

1,795

22,895 people attended the concert on both nights.

T: For 2 minutes with your partner draw a tape diagram. (Pause as they work. Circulate and encourage. One mode of delivery of instruction is to call two sets of partners to draw on the board while others work at their seats. Have the pairs then present their diagrams to the class.)

T: (After drawing.) Now how can you calculate to solve the problem?

S: We can find the number of people on Sunday night, and then add that number to the people on Saturday night.

T: Make an estimate of the solution. Explain your reasoning to your partner.

S: Rounding to the nearest thousand, the number of people on Saturday night was about 12,000. The number of people fewer on Sunday night can be rounded to 2,000, so the estimate for the number of people on Sunday is 10,000. 12,000 + 10,000 is 22,000.

T: Find the exact number of people who attended the concert on both nights. What is the exact sum?

S: 22,895.

Lesson 16: Solve two-step word problems using the standard subtraction algorithm fluently modeled with tape diagrams and assess the reasonableness of answers using rounding.

Date: 6/28/13

T: Compare the actual and estimated solutions. Is your answer reasonable?

S: Yes, because 22,895 is near our estimate of 22,000.

T: Be sure to write a statement of your solution.

Problem Set (10 minutes)

Students should do their personal best to complete the Problem Set within the allotted 10 minutes. For some classes, it may be appropriate to modify the assignment by specifying which problems they work on first. Some problems do not specify a method for solving. Students solve these problems using the RDW approach used for Application Problems.

Student Debrief (13 minutes)

Lesson Objective: Solve two-step word problems using the standard subtraction algorithm fluently modeled with tape diagrams and assess the reasonableness of answers using rounding.

The Student Debrief is intended to invite reflection and active processing of the total lesson experience.

Invite students to review their solutions for the Problem Set. They should check work by comparing answers with a partner before going over answers as a class. Look for misconceptions or misunderstandings that can be addressed in the Debrief. Guide students in a conversation to debrief the Problem Set and process the lesson. You may choose to use any combination of the questions below to lead the discussion.

- How did your estimate help you determine that your exact answer was correct in Problem 1?
- Why was the estimate so much smaller than the exact answer in Problem 1?
- In Problem 2, how close was your actual answer to your estimate?
- In Problem 3, to which place did you round? Why?
- How did your tape diagram help you solve Problem 5?

Lesson 16: Solve two-step word problems using the standard subtraction algorithm fluently modeled with tape diagrams and assess the reasonableness of answers using rounding.

Date: 6/28/13

1.E.43

© 2013 Common Core, Inc. All rights reserved. commoncore.org

- How do you determine what place value to round to when finding an estimate?
- What is the benefit of checking the reasonableness of your answer?
- Describe the difference between rounding and estimating.

Exit Ticket (3 minutes)

After the Student Debrief, instruct students to complete the Exit Ticket. A review of their work will help you assess the students' understanding of the concepts that were presented in the lesson today and plan more effectively for future lessons. You may read the questions aloud to the students.

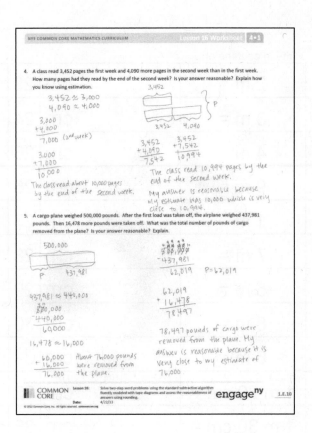

COMMON CORE™

Lesson 16: Solve two-step word problems using the standard subtraction algorithm fluently modeled with tape diagrams and assess the reasonableness of answers using rounding.

Date: 6/28/13

1.E.44

© 2013 Common Core, Inc. All rights reserved. commoncore.org

A

Write in centimeters.   # Correct _____

1	2 m =	cm	23	1 m 2 cm =	cm
2	3 m =	cm	24	1 m 3 cm =	cm
3	4 m =	cm	25	1 m 4 cm =	cm
4	9 m =	cm	26	1 m 7 cm =	cm
5	1 m =	cm	27	2 m 7 cm =	cm
6	7 m =	cm	28	3 m 7 cm =	cm
7	5 m =	cm	29	8 m 7 cm =	cm
8	8 m =	cm	30	8 m 4 cm =	cm
9	6 m =	cm	31	4 m 9 cm =	cm
10	1 m 20 cm =	cm	32	6 m 8 cm =	cm
11	1 m 30 cm =	cm	33	9 m 3 cm =	cm
12	1 m 40 cm =	cm	34	2 m 60 cm =	cm
13	1 m 90 cm =	cm	35	3 m 75 cm =	cm
14	1 m 95 cm =	cm	36	6 m 33 cm =	cm
15	1 m 85 cm =	cm	37	8 m 9 cm =	cm
16	1 m 84 cm =	cm	38	4 m 70 cm =	cm
17	1 m 73 cm =	cm	39	7 m 35 cm =	cm
18	1 m 62 cm =	cm	40	4 m 17 cm =	cm
19	2 m 62 cm =	cm	41	6 m 4 cm =	cm
20	7 m 62 cm =	cm	42	10 m 4 cm =	cm
21	5 m 27 cm =	cm	43	10 m 40 cm =	cm
22	3 m 87 cm =	cm	44	11 m 84 cm =	cm

© Bill Davidson

Lesson 16:   Solve two-step word problems using the standard subtraction
               algorithm fluently modeled with tape diagrams and assess the
               reasonableness of answers using rounding.
Date: 6/28/13

1.E.45

B

Improvement _____   # Correct _____

Write in centimeters.

#	Problem	Answer	#	Problem	Answer
1	1 m =	cm	23	1 m 1 cm =	cm
2	2 m =	cm	24	1 m 2 cm =	cm
3	3 m =	cm	25	1 m 3 cm =	cm
4	7 m =	cm	26	1 m 9 cm =	cm
5	5 m =	cm	27	2 m 9 cm =	cm
6	9 m =	cm	28	3 m 9 cm =	cm
7	4 m =	cm	29	7 m 9 cm =	cm
8	8 m =	cm	30	7 m 4 cm =	cm
9	6 m =	cm	31	4 m 8 cm =	cm
10	1 m 10 cm =	cm	32	6 m 3 cm =	cm
11	1 m 20 cm =	cm	33	9 m 5 cm =	cm
12	1 m 30 cm =	cm	34	2 m 50 cm =	cm
13	1 m 70 cm =	cm	35	3 m 85 cm =	cm
14	1 m 75 cm =	cm	36	6 m 31 cm =	cm
15	1 m 65 cm =	cm	37	6 m 7 cm =	cm
16	1 m 64 cm =	cm	38	4 m 60 cm =	cm
17	1 m 53 cm =	cm	39	7 m 25 cm =	cm
18	1 m 42 cm =	cm	40	4 m 13 cm =	cm
19	2 m 42 cm =	cm	41	6 m 2 cm =	cm
20	8 m 42 cm =	cm	42	10 m 3 cm =	cm
21	5 m 29 cm =	cm	43	10 m 30 cm =	cm
22	3 m 89 cm =	cm	44	11 m 48 cm =	cm

© Bill Davidson

Lesson 16:   Solve two-step word problems using the standard subtraction
            algorithm fluently modeled with tape diagrams and assess the
            reasonableness of answers using rounding.
Date: 6/28/13

1.E.46

Name _____   Date _____

Directions: Estimate first and then solve each problem. Model the problem with a tape diagram. Explain if your answer is reasonable.

1. On Monday, a farm sold 25,196 pounds of potatoes. On Tuesday, they sold 18,023 pounds. On Wednesday, they sold some more potatoes. In all, they sold 62,409 pounds of potatoes in the 3 days.

    a. About how many pounds of potatoes did the farm sell on Wednesday? Estimate by rounding each value to the nearest thousand and then compute.

    b. Find the precise number of pounds of potatoes sold on Wednesday.

    c. Is your precise answer reasonable? Compare your estimate from (a) to your answer from (b). Write a sentence to explain your reasoning.

COMMON CORE™

Lesson 16:   Solve two-step word problems using the standard subtraction
                 algorithm fluently modeled with tape diagrams and assess the
                 reasonableness of answers using rounding.
Date: 6/28/13

1.E.47

2. A gas station had two pumps. Pump A dispensed 241,752 gallons. Pump B dispensed 113,916 more gallons than Pump A.

    a. About how many gallons did both pumps dispense? Estimate by rounding each value to the nearest hundred thousand and then compute.

    b. Exactly how many gallons did both pumps dispense?

    c. Assess the reasonableness of your answer in (b). Use your estimate from (a) to explain.

3. Martin's car had 86,456 miles on it. Of that distance, Martin's wife drove 24,901 miles, and his son drove 7,997 miles. Martin drove the rest.

    a. About how many miles did Martin drive? Round each value to estimate.

    b. Exactly how many miles did Martin drive?

    c. Assess the reasonableness of your answer in (b). Use your estimate from (a) to explain.

COMMON CORE™   Lesson 16:   Solve two-step word problems using the standard subtraction
                     algorithm fluently modeled with tape diagrams and assess the   1.E.48
                     reasonableness of answers using rounding.
          Date: 6/28/13

© 2013 Common Core, Inc. All rights reserved. commoncore.org

4. A class read 3,452 pages the first week and 4,090 more pages in the second week than in the first week. How many pages had they read by the end of the second week? Is your answer reasonable? Explain how you know using estimation.

5. A cargo plane weighed 500,000 pounds. After the first load was taken off, the airplane weighed 437,981 pounds. Then 16,478 more pounds were taken off. What was the total number of pounds of cargo removed from the plane? Is your answer reasonable? Explain.

COMMON CORE™ | **Lesson 16:** Solve two-step word problems using the standard subtraction algorithm fluently modeled with tape diagrams and assess the reasonableness of answers using rounding. | **1.E.49**

Date: 6/28/13

© 2013 Common Core, Inc. All rights reserved. commoncore.org

Name _____   Date _____

Directions: Model each problem with a tape diagram. Estimate and then solve each problem. Explain if your answer is reasonable.

1. Quarterback Brett Favre passed for 71,838 yards between the years 1991 and 2011. His all-time high was 4,413 passing yards in one year. In his second highest year, he threw 4,212 passing yards.

    a. About how many passing yards did he throw in the remaining years? Estimate by rounding each value to the nearest thousand and then compute.

    b. Exactly how many passing yards did he throw in the remaining years?

    c. Assess the reasonableness of your answer in (b). Use your estimate from (a) to explain.

COMMON CORE™

Lesson 16:   Solve two-step word problems using the standard subtraction
             algorithm fluently modeled with tape diagrams and assess the
             reasonableness of answers using rounding.
Date: 6/28/13

1.E.50

Name _____   Date _____

Directions: Model each problem with a tape diagram. Estimate and then solve each problem. Explain if your answer is reasonable.

1. Zachary's final project for a college course took a semester to write and had 95,234 words. Zachary wrote 35,295 words the first month and 19,240 words the second month. How many words did he write during the remaining part of the semester?

    a. Round each value to the nearest ten thousand to estimate how many words Zachary wrote during the remaining part of the semester.

    b. Find the exact number of words written during the remaining part of the semester.

    c. Use your answer from (a) to explain why your answer in (b) is reasonable.

COMMON CORE™

Lesson 16: Solve two-step word problems using the standard subtraction algorithm fluently modeled with tape diagrams and assess the reasonableness of answers using rounding.

Date: 6/28/13

© 2013 Common Core, Inc. All rights reserved. commoncore.org

1.E.51

2. During the first quarter of the year, 351,875 people purchased a particular app for their smartphones. During the second quarter of the year, 101,949 fewer people downloaded the app than during the first quarter. How many downloads occurred during the two quarters of the year?

   a. Round each number to the nearest hundred thousand to estimate how many downloads occurred during the first two quarters of the year.

   b. Determine exactly how many downloads occurred during the first two quarters of the year.

   c. Determine if your answer is reasonable. Explain.

3. A local store was having a two-week Back to School sale. They started the sale with 36,390 notebooks. During the first week of the sale, 7,424 notebooks were sold. During the second week of the sale, 8,967 notebooks were sold. How many notebooks were left at the end of the two weeks? Is your answer reasonable? Explain how you know using rounding.

Lesson 16:	Solve two-step word problems using the standard subtraction algorithm fluently modeled with tape diagrams and assess the reasonableness of answers using rounding.	1.E.52
Date:	6/28/13	

Topic F

Addition and Subtraction Word Problems

4.OA.3, 4.NBT.1, 4.NBT.2, 4.NBT.4

Focus Standard:	4.OA.3	Solve multistep word problems posed with whole numbers and having whole-number answers using the four operations, including problems in which remainders must be interpreted. Represent these problems using equations with a letter standing for the unknown quantity. Assess the reasonableness of answers using mental computation and estimation strategies including rounding.
Instructional Days:	3	
Coherence -Links from:	G3–M2	Place Value and Problem Solving with Units of Measure
-Links to:	G5–M1	Place Value and Decimal Fractions

The module culminates with multi-step addition and subtraction word problems in Topic F (**4.OA.3**). The format for the Concept Development is different from the traditional script. The Problem Set will facilitate the problems and discussion, as they are used during the Concept Development, instead of following instruction. Throughout the module, tape diagrams are used to model word problems and in this topic, students will continue to use them to solve additive comparative word problems. Students continue using a variable to represent an unknown quantity.   To culminate the module, students are given tape diagrams or equations and encouraged to use creativity and the mathematics learned during this module to write their own word problems to solve using place value understanding and the algorithms for addition and subtraction. The module facilitates deeper comprehension and supports the reasonableness in an answer. Solving multi-step word problems using multiplication and division will be addressed in later modules.

A Teaching Sequence Towards Mastery of Addition and Subtraction Word Problems

Objective 1: Solve additive compare word problems modeled with tape diagrams.
(Lesson 17)

Objective 2: Solve multi-step word problems modeled with tape diagrams and assess the reasonableness of answers using rounding.
(Lesson 18)

Objective 3: Create and solve multi-step word problems from given tape diagrams and equations.
(Lesson 19)

	Topic F:	Addition and Subtraction Word Problems
	Date:	6/28/13

1.F.2

Lesson 17

Objective: Solve additive compare word problems modeled with tape diagrams.

Suggested Lesson Structure

■ Fluency Practice	(10 minutes)
■ Application Problems	(8 minutes)
■ Concept Development	(35 minutes)
■ Student Debrief	(7 minutes)
Total Time	**(60 minutes)**

Fluency Practice (10 minutes)

- Change Place Value **4.NBT.2**   (5 minutes)
- Convert Units **4.MD.1**   (5 minutes)

Change Place Value (5 minutes)

Materials: (S) Personal white board, place value chart to the millions

Note: Reviewing this fluency will help students work towards mastery of using place value skills to add and subtract different units.

    T: (Project place value chart to the millions place. Write 4 hundred thousands, 6 ten thousands, 3 thousands, 2 hundreds, 6 tens, 5 ones.) On your personal white boards, write the number.

    S: (Students do so.)

    T: Show 100 more.

    S: (Students write 463,365.)

Possible further sequence: 10,000 less, 100,000 more, 1 less, 10 more.

    T: (Write 400 + 90 + 3 =____). On your place value chart, write the number.

Possible further sequence: 7,000 + 300 + 80 + 5; 20,000 + 700,000 + 5 + 80; 30,000 + 600,000 + 3 + 20.

Convert Units (5 minutes)

Note: Reviewing these unit conversions that were learned in third grade will help prepare the students to solve problems with kilometers and meters in Topic A of Module 2.

    T: (Write 1 km = ___ m.) How many meters are in a kilometer?

    S: 1 km = 1,000 m.

	Lesson 17:	Solve additive compare word problems modeled with tape diagrams.	
	Date:	6/28/13	1.F.3

© 2013 Common Core, Inc. All rights reserved. **commoncore.org**

Repeat process for 2 km, 3 km, 8 km, 8 km 500 m, 7 km 500 m, and 4 km 250 m.

> T: (Write 1,000 m = ___ km.) Say the answer.
>
> S: 1,000 m = 1 km.
>
> T: (Write 1,500 m = ___ km ___ m.) Say the answer.
>
> S: 1,500 m = 1 km 500 m.

Repeat process for 2,500 m, 3,500 m, 9,500 m, and 7,250 m.

Application Problem (8 minutes)

A bakery used 12,674 kg of flour. Of that, 1,802 kg was whole wheat and 888 kg was rice flour. The rest was all-purpose flour. How much all-purpose flour did they use? Solve and check the reasonableness of your answer.

Note: This problem leads well into today's lesson and bridges as it goes back into the work from Lesson 16.

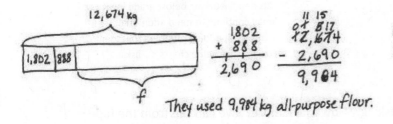

Concept Development (35 minutes)

Materials: (S) Problem Set

Suggested Delivery of Instruction for Solving Topic F's Word Problems

1. Model the problem.

Have two pairs of students who you think can be successful with modeling the problem work at the board while the others work independently or in pairs at their seats. Review the following questions before solving the first problem.

- Can you draw something?
- What can you draw?
- What conclusions can you make from your drawing?

As students work, circulate. Reiterate the questions above.

After 2 minutes, have the two pairs of students share *only* their labeled diagrams.

For about 1 minute, have the demonstrating students receive and respond to feedback and questions from their peers.

Lesson 17:	Solve additive compare word problems modeled with tape diagrams.	1.F.4
Date:	6/28/13	

2. Calculate to solve and write a statement.

Give everyone 2 minutes to finish work on that question, sharing their work, and thinking with a peer. All should then write their equations and statements of the answer.

3. Assess the solution for reasonableness.

Give students 1–2 minutes to assess and explain the reasonableness of their solution.

Note: In Lessons 17–19, the Problem Set will be comprised of word problems from the lesson and is therefore to be used during the lesson itself.

Problem 1

Solve a single-step word problems using how much more.

Sean's school raised $32,587. Leslie's school raised $18,749. How much more money did Sean's school raise?

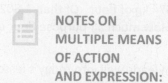
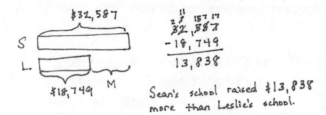
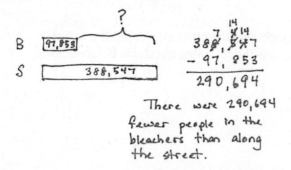

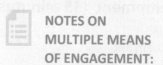
NOTES ON MULTIPLE MEANS OF ACTION AND EXPRESSION:

Students working below grade level may continue to need additional support in adding numbers together using place value charts or disks.

Support them in realizing that though the question is asking, "How much more?" we can see from the tape diagram that the unknown is a missing part, therefore we subtract to find the answer.

Problem 2

Solve a single-step word problem using how many fewer.

At a parade, 97,853 people sat in bleachers. 388,547 people stood along the street. How many fewer people were in the bleachers than standing along the street?

NOTES ON MULTIPLE MEANS OF ENGAGEMENT:

Challenge students to think about how reasonableness can be associated with rounding. If the actual answer does not round to the estimate, does it mean that the answer is not reasonable?

Ask students to explain their thinking. (For example, 376 – 134 = 242. Rounding to the nearest hundred would result with an estimate of 400 – 100 = 300. The actual answer of 242 rounds to 200, not 300.)

Circulate and support students to realize that the unknown is a missing part. Encourage them to write a statement using the word *fewer* when talking about separate things. For example, I have *fewer* apples than you do but *less* juice.

Lesson 17:   Solve additive compare word problems modeled with tape
diagrams.
Date: 6/28/13

1.F.5

Problem 3

Solve a two-step problem using how much more.

A pair of hippos weighed 5,201 kg together. The female weighed 2,038 kg. How much more did the male weigh than the female?

IP.2

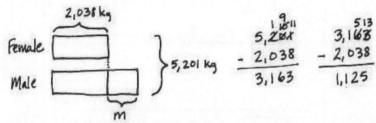

Many students will want to draw this as a single bar showing the combined weight to start. That works. However, the second step will most likely require a new double bar to compare the weights of the male and female. If no one comes up with the model pictured, you can show it quickly. Students generally do not choose to draw a bracket with the known total to the side until they are very familiar with two-step comparison models. However, be aware that students will have modeled this problem type since Grade 2.

Problem 4

Solve a three-step problem using how much longer.

A copper wire was 240 m long. After 60 m was cut off, it was double the length of a steel wire. How much longer was the copper wire than the steel wire at first?

$$240 - 60 = 180$$
$$180 \div 2 = 90$$
$$240 - 90 = 150$$

The copper wire was 150 m longer than the steel wire at first.

> **NOTES ON MULTIPLE MEANS OF ACTION AND EXPRESSION:**
>
> For students who may find Problem 4 challenging, remind them of the work done earlier in this module with multiples of 10. For example, 180 is ten times as much as 18. If 18 divided by 2 is 9, then 180 divided by 2 is 90.

T: Read the problem, draw a model, write equations both to estimate and calculate precisely and write a statement. I'll give you 5 minutes.

Circulate, using the bulleted questions to guide students. Encourage the students when they get stuck to focus on what they can learn from their drawing:

- Show me the copper wire at first.
- Show me in your model what happened to the copper wire.
- Show me in your model what you know about the steel wire.

Lesson 17:	Solve additive compare word problems modeled with tape diagrams.	1.F.6
Date:	6/28/13	

- What are you comparing? Where is that difference in your model?

Notice the number size is quite small here. The calculations are not the issue but rather the relationships. Students will eventually solve similar problems with larger numbers but begin here at a simple level numerically.

Problem Set

Please note that the Problem Sets in Topic F are comprised of the lesson's problems as stated at the introduction of the lesson.

For some classes, it may be appropriate to modify the assignment by specifying which problems they work on first. Some problems do not specify a method for solving. Students solve these problems using the RDW approach used for Application Problems.

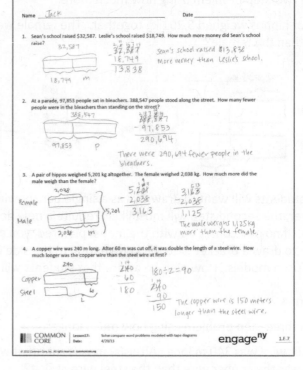

Student Debrief (7 minutes)

Lesson Objective: Solve additive compare word problems modeled with tape diagrams.

The Student Debrief is intended to invite reflection and active processing of the total lesson experience.

Invite students to review their solutions for the Problem Set. They should check work by comparing answers with a partner before going over answers as a class. Look for misconceptions or misunderstandings that can be addressed in the Debrief. Guide students in a conversation to debrief the Problem Set and process the lesson. You may choose to use any combination of the questions below to lead the discussion.

- How are your tape diagrams for Problem 1 and Problem 2 similar?
- How did your tape diagrams vary across all problems?
- How did drawing a double tape diagram instead of a single tape diagram in Problem 3 help to better visualize the problem?
- What was most challenging about drawing the tape diagram from Problem 4? What helped you to find the best diagram to solve the problem?
- What different ways are there to draw a tape diagram to solve comparative problems?
- What does the word compare mean?
- What phrases do you notice repeated through many of today's problems that help you to see the problem as a comparative problem?

Exit Ticket (3 minutes)

After the Student Debrief, instruct students to complete the Exit Ticket. A review of their work will help you assess the students' understanding of the concepts that were presented in the lesson today and plan more effectively for future lessons. You may read the questions aloud to the students.

Name _____   Date _____

Directions: Model each problem using a tape diagram. Solve using numbers and words.

1. Sean's school raised $32,587. Leslie's school raised $18,749. How much more money did Sean's school raise?

2. At a parade, 97,853 people sat in bleachers and 388,547 people stood along the street. How many fewer people were in the bleachers than standing on the street?

3. A pair of hippos weighed 5,201 kg together. The female weighed 2,038 kg. How much more did the male weigh than the female?

4. A copper wire was 240 m long. After 60 m was cut off, it was double the length of a steel wire. How much longer was the copper wire than the steel wire at first?

Lesson 17:	Solve additive compare word problems modeled with tape diagrams.
Date:	6/28/13

1.F.9

Name _____   Date _____

Directions: Estimate, then solve the following problem modeling with a tape diagram.

1. A mixture of 2 chemicals measures 1,034 ml. It contains some of Chemical A and 755 ml of Chemical B.
    How much less of Chemical A than Chemical B was in the mixture?

Name _____   Date _____

1. Gavin has 1,094 toy building blocks. Avery has only 816 toy building blocks. How many more building blocks does Gavin have?

2. Container A and B hold 11,875 L of water altogether. Container B holds 2,391 L more than container A holds. How much water does Container A hold?

3. A piece of yellow yarn was 230 inches long. After 90 inches had been cut from it, the piece of yellow yarn was twice as long as a piece of blue yarn. How much longer than the blue yarn was the yellow yarn at first?

Lesson 18

Objective: Solve multi-step word problems modeled with tape diagrams and assess the reasonableness of answers using rounding.

Suggested Lesson Structure

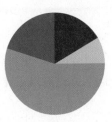

■ Fluency Practice   (10 minutes)
■ Application Problem   (5 minutes)
■ Concept Development   (33 minutes)
■ Student Debrief   (12 minutes)

  Total Time   **(60 minutes)**

Fluency Practice (10 minutes)

- Number Patterns **4.OA.5**   (5 minutes)
- Convert Units **4.MD.1**   (5 minutes)

Number Patterns (5 minutes)

Materials: (S) Personal white boards

Note: This fluency bolsters students' place value understanding and helps them apply these skills to a variety of concepts.

    T: (Project 40,100   50,100   60,100   ____.) What is the place value of the digit that's changing?
    S: Ten thousand.
    T: Count with me saying the value of the digit I'm pointing to.
    S: (Point at the ten thousand digit as students count.) 40,000, 50,000, 60,000.
    T: On your boards write what number would come after 60,100.
    S: (Students write 70,100.)

Repeat with the following possible sequence: 82,030, 72,030, 62,030, ___ ; 215,003, 216,003, 217,003, ___ ; 943,612, 943,512, 943,412, ___ ; and 372,435, 382,435, 392,435, ___.

Convert Units (5 minutes)

Materials: (S) Personal white boards

Note: Reviewing these unit conversions that were learned in third grade will help prepare the students solve problems with kilometers and meters in Topic A of Module 2.

Lesson 18:   Solve multi-step word problems modeled with tape diagrams and
               assess the reasonableness of answers using rounding.
Date: 6/28/13

1.F.12

T: Count by 200 meters, starting at 200 meters. When you get to 1000 meters, say 1 kilometer.

S: 200 m, 400 m, 600 m, 800 m, 1 km, 1,200 m, 1,400 m, 1,600 m, 1,800 m, and 2 km.

Repeat process, this time pulling out the kilometer (e.g., 1 km 200 m, 1 km 400 m).

T: (Write 1,300 m = ___ km ___ m.) On your boards, fill-in the blanks.

S: (Students regroup 1,300 m into 1 km 300 m.)

Repeat process for 1,003 m, 1,750 m, 3,450 m, and 7,030 m.

Application Problem (5 minutes)

In all, 30,436 people went skiing in February and January. 16,009 went skiing in February. How many fewer people went skiing in February than in February?

$$
\begin{array}{l}
D \quad \boxed{16,009} \\
F \quad \boxed{} \\
\qquad\qquad ?
\end{array}
\left.\begin{array}{l} \\ \\ \\ \end{array}\right\} \quad 30,436
\qquad
\begin{array}{r}
{}^{2\,10}\ {}^{2\,16} \\
\cancel{3\cancel{0},4\cancel{3}\cancel{6}} \\
-16,009 \\
\hline
14,427
\end{array}
\qquad
\begin{array}{r}
{}^{5\,9\,10} \\
\cancel{16,\cancel{0}\cancel{0}9} \\
-14,427 \\
\hline
1,582
\end{array}
$$

In February 1,582 fewer people went skiing than in January.

Note: This problem reviews content from the prior lesson and is a comparison subtraction problem.

Concept Development (33 minutes)

Materials: (S) Student Problem Set

Suggested Delivery of Instruction for Solving Topic F's Word Problems

1. Model the problem.

Have two pairs of students who you think can be successful with modeling the problem work at the board while the others work independently or in pairs at their seats. Review the following questions before beginning the first problem.

- Can you draw something?
- What can you draw?
- What conclusions can you make from your drawing?

As students work, circulate. Reiterate the questions above. After 2 minutes, have the two pairs of students share *only* their labeled diagrams. For about 1 minute, have the demonstrating students receive and respond to feedback and questions from their peers.

Lesson 18:	Solve multi-step word problems modeled with tape diagrams and
Date:	assess the reasonableness of answers using rounding.
	6/28/13

1.F.13

2. Calculate to solve and write a statement.

Give everyone 2 minutes to finish work on that question, sharing their work and thinking with a peer. All should then write their equations and statements of the answer.

3. Assess the solution for reasonableness.

Give students 1–2 minutes to assess and explain the reasonableness of their solution.

Note: In Lessons 17–19, the Problem Set will be comprised of the word problems from the lesson and is therefore to be used during the lesson itself.

Problem 1

Solve a multi-step word problem, requiring addition and subtraction, using a tape diagram, and checking the reasonableness of the answer using estimation.

In one year, a factory used 11,650 meters of cotton, 4,950 fewer meters of silk than cotton, and 3,500 fewer meters of wool than silk. How many meters in all were used of the three fabrics?

This problem is a step forward for students as they subtract to find the amount of wool from the amount of silk. Students also might subtract the sum of 4,950 and 3,500 from 11,650 to find the meters of wool and add that to the amount of silk. It's a longer method but makes sense. As you circulate, look for other alternate strategies which can be quickly mentioned or explored more deeply as per your professional judgment. Be advised, however, not to emphasize creativity but rather analysis and efficiency. Ingenious short cuts might be highlighted.

After the students have solved the problem, ask them to check their answer for reasonableness.

T: How can you know if 21,550 is a reasonable answer? Discuss with your partner.

S: Well, I can see by looking at the diagram that the amount of wool fits in the part that the silk is missing. So the answer is a little less than double 12 thousand, so our answer makes sense.

S: Another way to think about it is that 11,650 can be rounded to 12 thousand. 12 thousand plus 7 thousand for the silk since 12 thousand minus 5 thousand is 7 thousand plus about 4 thousand for the wool, that's 23 thousand.

Problem 2

Solve an additive multi-step word problem using a tape diagram, checking the reasonableness of the answer using estimation.

The shop sold 12,789 chocolate and 9,324 cookie dough cones. They sold 1,078 more peanut butter cones than cookie dough cones and 999 more vanilla cones than chocolate cones. What was the total number of ice cream cones sold?

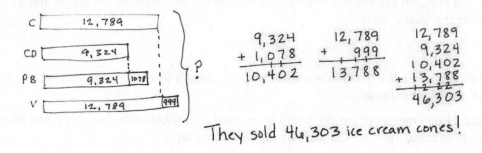

The solution above shows calculating the total number of cones of each flavor and then adding. Students may also add like units before adding the extra parts.

After the students have solved the problem, ask them to check their answer for reasonableness.

MP.3

T: How can you know if 46,303 is a reasonable answer? Discuss with your partner.

S: By looking at the tape diagram, I can see we have 2 thirteen thousands. That's 26 thousand. We have 2 nine thousands, that's 26 and 18 is 44. Plus about 2 thousand more, that's 46 thousand. That's close.

S: Another way to see it is that I can kind of see 2 thirteen thousands and the little extra pieces with the peanut butter make 11 thousand. That is 37 thousand plus 9 thousand from cookie dough is 46 thousand. That's close.

Problem 3

Solve a multi-step word problem, requiring addition and subtraction, modeled with a tape diagram, checking the reasonableness of the answer using estimation.

In the first week of June, a restaurant sold 10,345 omelets. The second week, they sold 1,096 fewer omelets than the first week. The third week, they sold 2 thousand more than the first week. The fourth week, they sold 2 thousand fewer than the first week. How many omelets did they sell in all in June?

Week 1 | 10,345
Week 2 | ____ 1096
Week 3 | 10,345 | 2,000
Week 4 | ____ 2,000

?

$$\begin{array}{r} 10,345 \\ 10,345 \\ + 10,345 \\ \hline 31,035 \end{array}$$

$$\begin{array}{r} 10,3\overset{13}{\cancel{4}}\overset{15}{\cancel{5}} \\ - 1,096 \\ \hline 9,249 \end{array}$$

$$\begin{array}{r} 31,035 \\ + 9,249 \\ \hline 40,284 \end{array}$$

The restaurant sold 40,284 burgers in June.

COMMON CORE™

Lesson 18:   Solve multi-step word problems modeled with tape diagrams and
assess the reasonableness of answers using rounding.
Date: 6/28/13

1.F.15

This problem is interesting because 2 thousand more and 2 thousand less mean that there is one more unit of 10,345. We therefore simply add in the omelets from week 2.

T: How can you know if 40,284 is a reasonable answer? Discuss with your partner.

S: By looking at the tape diagram, it's easy to see it is like 3 ten thousands plus 9 thousand, that's 39 thousand. That is close to our answer.

S: Another way to see it is just rounding one week at a time starting at week one, 10 thousand plus 9 thousand plus 12 thousand plus 8 thousand. That's 39 thousand.

Problem Set

Please note that the Problem Set in Topic F is comprised of the lesson's problems as stated at the introduction of the lesson.

For some classes, it may be appropriate to modify the assignment by specifying which problems they work on first. Some problems do not specify a method for solving. Students solve these problems using the RDW approach used for Application Problems.

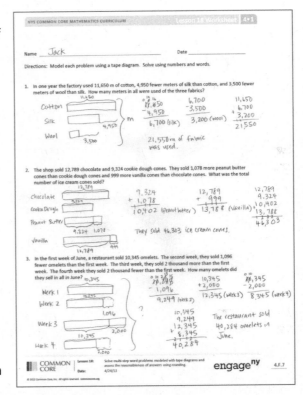

Student Debrief (12 minutes)

Lesson Objective: Solve multi-step word problems modeled with tape diagrams and assess the reasonableness of answers using rounding.

The Student Debrief is intended to invite reflection and active processing of the total lesson experience.

Invite students to review their solutions for the Problem Set. They should check work by comparing answers with a partner before going over answers as a class. Look for misconceptions or misunderstandings that can be addressed in the Debrief. Guide students in a conversation to debrief the Problem Set and process the lesson. You may choose to use any combination of the questions below to lead the discussion.

- How are the problems alike? How are they different?
- How was your solution the same and different from those that were demonstrated?
- Why is there more than one right way to solve, for example, Problem 3?
- Did you see other solutions that surprised you or made you see the problem differently?
- In Problem 1, was the part unknown or the total unknown? What about in Problems 2 and 3?
- Why is it helpful to assess for reasonableness after solving?
- How were the tape diagrams helpful to us in estimating to test for reasonableness? Why is that?

Lesson 18:   Solve multi-step word problems modeled with tape diagrams and
Date: assess the reasonableness of answers using rounding.
            6/28/13

Exit Ticket (3 minutes)

After the Student Debrief, instruct students to complete the Exit Ticket. A review of their work will help you assess the students' understanding of the concepts that were presented in the lesson today and plan more effectively for future lessons. You may read the questions aloud to the students.

COMMON CORE™

Lesson 18:
Date:

Solve multi-step word problems modeled with tape diagrams and assess the reasonableness of answers using rounding.
6/28/13

1.F.17

Name _____   Date _____

Directions: Model each problem using a tape diagram. Solve using numbers and words.

1. In one year the factory used 11,650 meter of cotton, 4,950 fewer meters of silk than cotton, and 3,500 fewer meters of wool than silk. How many meters in all were used of the three fabrics?

2. The shop sold 12,789 chocolate and 9,324 cookie dough cones. They sold 1,078 more peanut butter cones than cookie dough cones and 999 more vanilla cones than chocolate cones. What was the total number of ice cream cones sold?

3. In the first week of June, a restaurant sold 10,345 omelets. The second week, they sold 1,096 fewer omelets than the first week. The third week, they sold 2 thousand more than the first week. The fourth week, they sold 2 thousand fewer than the first week. How many omelets did they sell in all in June?

COMMON CORE™   Lesson 18:   Solve multi-step word problems modeled with tape diagrams and   1.F.18
assess the reasonableness of answers using rounding.
Date: 6/28/13

© 2013 Common Core, Inc. All rights reserved. commoncore.org

Name _____   Date _____

Directions: Draw a tape diagram to represent the problem. Use numbers and words to explain your thinking.

1. Park A covers an area of 4,926 square kilometers. It is 1,845 square kilometers larger than Park B.
    Park C is 4,006 square kilometers larger than the Park A.

    a. What is the area of all three parks?

    b. Assess the reasonableness of your answer.

Lesson 18:   Solve multi-step word problems modeled with tape diagrams and
               assess the reasonableness of answers using rounding.   1.F.19
Date: 6/28/13

© 2013 Common Core, Inc. All rights reserved. commoncore.org

Name _____   Date _____

Directions: Model each problem using a tape diagram. Solve using numbers and words.

1. There were 22,869 children, 49,563 men, and 2,872 more women than men at the fair. How many people were at the fair?

2. Number A is 4,676. Number B is 10,043 greater than A. Number C is 2,610 less than B. What is the total value of numbers A, B, and C?

3. A store sold a total of 21,650 balls. It sold 11,795 baseballs. It sold 4,150 fewer basketballs than baseballs. The rest of the balls sold were footballs. How many footballs did the store sell?

COMMON CORE™   Lesson 18:   Solve multi-step word problems modeled with tape diagrams and assess the reasonableness of answers using rounding.   **1.F.20**

Date: 6/28/13

Lesson 19

Objective: Create and solve multi-step word problems from given tape diagrams and equations.

Suggested Lesson Structure

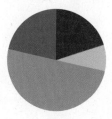

■ Fluency Practice   (12 minutes)

■ Application Problem   (5 minutes)

■ Concept Development   (30 minutes)

■ Student Debrief   (13 minutes)

   Total Time   **(60 minutes)**

Fluency Practice (12 minutes)

▪ Convert Meters to Kilometers and Meters **4.MD.1**   (8 minutes)

▪ Convert Units **4.MD.1**   (4 minutes)

Sprint: Convert Meters to Kilometers and Meters (8 minutes)

Materials: (S) Convert Meters to Kilometers and Meters Sprint

Note: Reviewing unit conversions that were learned in third grade will help prepare the students to solve problems with meters and kilometers in Topic A of Module 2.

Convert Units (4 minutes)

Note: Reviewing unit conversions that were learned in third grade will help prepare the students solve problems with centimeters and meters in Topic A of Module 2.

Materials: (S) Personal white boards

    T: (Write 1 m = ___ cm.) How many centimeters are in a meter?
    S: 1 m = 100 cm.

Repeat process for 2 m, 3 m, 8 m, 8 m 50 cm, 7 m 50 cm, and 4 m 25 cm.

    T: (Write 100 cm = ___ m.) Say the answer.
    S: 100 m = 1 m.
    T: (Write 150 cm = ___ m ___ cm.) Say the answer.
    S: 150 cm = 1 m 50 cm. Repeat process for 250 cm, 350 cm, 950 cm, and 725 cm.

Application Problem (5 minutes)

For Jordan to get to his grandparents' house, he has to travel through Albany and Plattsburgh. From Jordan's house to Albany is 189 miles. From Albany to Plattsburgh is 161 miles. If the total distance of the trip is 508 miles, how far from Plattsburgh do Jordan's grandparents live?

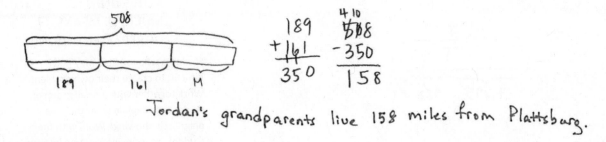

Note: This problem reviews two-step problems from the previous lessons.

Concept Development (30 minutes)

Materials: (S) Problem Set

Suggested Delivery of Instruction for Lesson 19's Word Problem.

1. Draw the labeled tape diagram on the board and give the students the context. Have them write a story problem based on the tape diagram.

Have two pairs of students who you think can be successful with writing a problem work at the board while the others work independently or in pairs at their seats. Review the following questions before beginning the first problem.

- What story makes sense with the diagram?
- What question will I ask in my word problem?

As students work, circulate. Reiterate the questions above.

After 2 minutes, have the two pairs of students share their stories.

For about 1 minute, have the demonstrating students receive and respond to feedback and questions from their peers.

2. Calculate to solve and write a statement.

Give everyone 2 minutes to exchange stories, calculate, and make a statement of the answer.

3. Assess the solution for reasonableness.

Give students 1–2 minutes to assess and explain the reasonableness of their solution.

Lesson 19:   Create and solve multi-step word problems from given tape
                diagrams and equations.
Date: 6/28/13

© 2013 Common Core, Inc. All rights reserved. commoncore.org

1.F.22

Note: In Lessons 17–19, the Problem Set will be comprised of the word problems from the lesson and is therefore to be used during the lesson itself.

Problem 1

Create and solve a simple two-step word problem from the tape diagram below.

Suggested context: People at a football game.

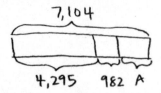

**NOTES ON
MULTIPLE MEANS
OF REPRESENTATION:**

Students who are ELLs may find it difficult to create their own problem. Work together with a small group of students to explain what the tape diagram is showing. Work with the students to write information into the tape diagram. Discuss what is known and unknown. Together, build a question based on the discussion.

Problem 2

Create and solve a two-step addition word problem from the tape diagram below.

Suggested context: Cost of two houses.

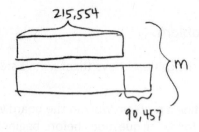

Problem 3

Create and solve a three-step word problem involving addition and subtraction from the tape diagram below.

Suggested context: Weight in kilograms of three different whales.

MP.2

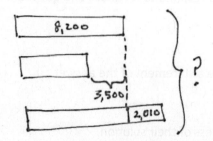

**NOTES ON
MULTIPLE MEANS
OF ACTION
AND REPRESENTATION:**

Students below grade level may struggle with the task of creating their own problems. These students may benefit from working together in a partnership with another student. First, encourage them to design a tape diagram showing the known parts, the unknown part, and the whole. Second, encourage them to create a word problem based on the diagram.

COMMON CORE™

Lesson 19:   Create and solve multi-step word problems from given tape
              diagrams and equations.
Date: 6/28/13

1.F.23

Problem 4

Students use equations to model and solve multi-step word problems.

Display the equation 5,233 + 3,094 + k = 12,946.

T: Draw a tape diagram that models this equation.

T: Compare with your partner. Then create a word problem that uses the numbers from the equation. Remember to first create a context, write a statement about the total and a question about the unknown. Then you can tell the rest of the information.

Students work independently. Students can share problems in partners to solve or select word problems to solve as a class.

Problem Set

Please note that the Problem Set in Topic F is comprised of the lesson's problems as stated at the introduction of the lesson.

For some classes, it may be appropriate to modify the assignment by specifying which problems they work on first. Some problems do not specify a method for solving. Students solve these problems using the RDW approach used for Application Problems.

Student Debrief (13 minutes)

Lesson Objective: Create and solve multi-step word problems from given tape diagrams and equations.

The Student Debrief is intended to invite reflection and active processing of the total lesson experience.

Invite students to review their solutions for the Problem Set. They should check work by comparing answers with a partner before going over answers as a class. Look for misconceptions or misunderstandings that can be addressed in the Debrief.

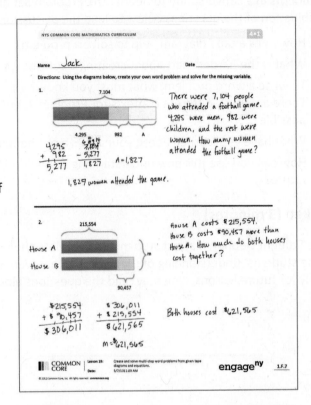

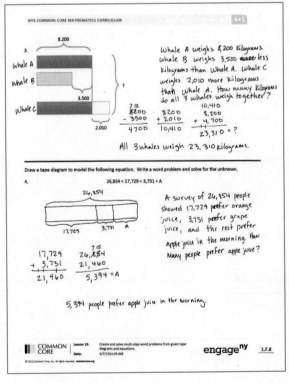

Lesson 19: Create and solve multi-step word problems from given tape diagrams and equations.
Date: 6/28/13

© 2013 Common Core, Inc. All rights reserved. commoncore.org

1.F.24

Guide students in a conversation to debrief the Problem Set and process the lesson. You may choose to use any combination of the questions below to lead the discussion.

- How does a tape diagram help to solve a problem?
- What is the hardest part about creating a context for a word problem?
- To write a word problem, what must you know?
  There are many different contexts for Problem 2, but everyone found the same answer. How is that possible?
- What have you learned about yourself as a mathematician over the past module?
- How can you use this new understanding of addition, subtraction, and solving word problems in the future?

Exit Ticket (3 minutes)

After the Student Debrief, instruct students to complete the Exit Ticket. A review of their work will help you assess the students' understanding of the concepts that were presented in the lesson today and plan more effectively for future lessons. You may read the questions aloud to the students.

COMMON CORE™　　**Lesson 19:**　　Create and solve multi-step word problems from given tape diagrams and equations.

Date:　　6/28/13

1.F.25

A

Correct _____

Write in kilometers and meters.

1	2,000 m =	km	m	23	3,800 m =	km	m
2	3,000 m =	km	m	24	4,770 m =	km	m
3	4,000 m =	km	m	25	4,807 m =	km	m
4	9,000 m =	km	m	26	5,065 m =	km	m
5	6,000 m =	km	m	27	5,040 m =	km	m
6	1,000 m =	km	m	28	6,007 m =	km	m
7	8,000 m =	km	m	29	2,003 m =	km	m
8	5,000 m =	km	m	30	1,090 m =	km	m
9	7,000 m =	km	m	31	1,055 m =	km	m
10	6,100 m =	km	m	32	9,404 m =	km	m
11	6,110 m =	km	m	33	9,330 m =	km	m
12	6,101 m =	km	m	34	3,400 m =	km	m
13	6,010 m =	km	m	35	4,000 m + 2,000 m =	km	m
14	6,011 m =	km	m	36	5,000 m + 3,000 m =	km	m
15	6,001 m =	km	m	37	4,000 m + 4,000 m =	km	m
16	8,002 m =	km	m	38	8 x 7,000 m =	km	m
17	8,020 m =	km	m	39	49,000 m ÷ 7 =	km	m
18	8,200 m =	km	m	40	16,000 m x 5 =	km	m
19	8,022 m =	km	m	41	63,000 m ÷ 7 =	km	m
20	8,220 m =	km	m	42	17 x 4,000 m =	km	m
21	8,222 m =	km	m	43	13,000 m x 5 =	km	m
22	7,256 m =	km	m	44	84,000 m ÷ 7 =	km	m

© Bill Davidson

Lesson 19: Create and solve multi-step word problems from given tape diagrams and equations.

Date: 6/28/13

1.F.26

B

Improvement _____   # Correct _____

Write in kilometers and meters.

#		km	m	#		km	m
1	1,000 m =	km	m	23	2,700 m =	km	m
2	2,000 m =	km	m	24	3,660 m =	km	m
3	3,000 m =	km	m	25	3,706 m =	km	m
4	8,000 m =	km	m	26	4,095 m =	km	m
5	6,000 m =	km	m	27	4,030 m =	km	m
6	9,000 m =	km	m	28	5,006 m =	km	m
7	4,000 m =	km	m	29	3,004 m =	km	m
8	7,000 m =	km	m	30	2,010 m =	km	m
9	5,000 m =	km	m	31	2,075 m =	km	m
10	5,100 m =	km	m	32	1,504 m =	km	m
11	5,110 m =	km	m	33	1,440 m =	km	m
12	5,101 m =	km	m	34	4,500 m =	km	m
13	5,010 m =	km	m	35	3,000 m + 2,000 m =	km	m
14	5,011 m =	km	m	36	4,000 m + 3,000 m =	km	m
15	5,001 m =	km	m	37	5,000 m + 4,000 m =	km	m
16	7,002 m =	km	m	38	9 x 8,000 m =	km	m
17	7,020 m =	km	m	39	64,000 m ÷ 8 =	km	m
18	7,200 m =	km	m	40	17,000 m x 5 =	km	m
19	7,022 m =	km	m	41	54,000 m ÷ 6 =	km	m
20	7,220 m =	km	m	42	18,000 m x 4 =	km	m
21	7,222 m =	km	m	43	14 x 5,000 m =	km	m
22	4,378 m =	km	m	44	96,000 m ÷ 8 =	km	m

© Bill Davidson

COMMON CORE™ Lesson 19:   Create and solve multi-step word problems from given tape diagrams and equations.
Date: 6/28/13

1.F.27

Name _____   Date _____

Directions: Using the diagrams below, create your own word problem and solve for the missing variable.

1.

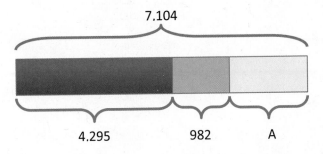

2.

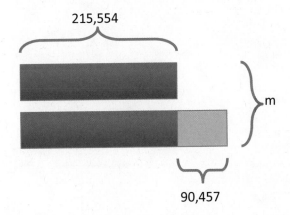

COMMON CORE™   Lesson 19:   Create and solve multi-step word problems from given tape
                                    diagrams and equations.   1.F.28
                     Date: 6/28/13

© 2013 Common Core, Inc. All rights reserved. **commoncore.org**

3.

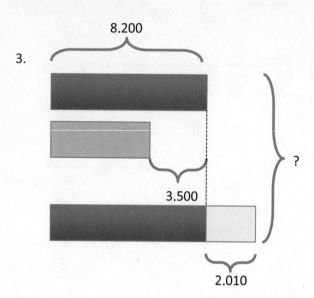

8.200

3.500

?

2.010

Draw a tape diagram to model the following equation. Write a word problem and solve for the unknown.

4.   26,854 = 17,729 + 3,731 + A

Lesson 19:   Create and solve multi-step word problems from given tape
             diagrams and equations.
Date: 6/28/13

1.F.29

© 2013 Common Core, Inc. All rights reserved. commoncore.org

Name _____   Date _____

Directions: Using the diagram below, create your own word problem and solve for the missing variable.

1.

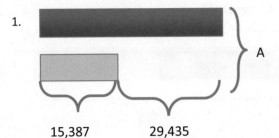

15,387   29,435

_____

Directions: Using the equation below, draw a tape diagram and create your own word problem.
Solve for the missing variable.

2. $248{,}798 = 113{,}205 + A + 99{,}937$

COMMON CORE | Lesson 19:   Create and solve multi-step word problems from given tape   **1.F.30**
                  | diagrams and equations.
                  | Date: 6/28/13

© 2013 Common Core, Inc. All rights reserved. commoncore.org

Name _____   Date _____

Directions: Using the diagrams below, create your own word problem to solve for the missing variable.

1.   At the local botanical gardens, there are _____

Redwoods and _____ Cypress trees.

There are a total of _____ Redwood,

Cypress, and Dogwood trees.

How many _____

_____

_____?

Redwood   Cypress   Dogwood

| 6,294 | 3,849 | A |

12,115

2.   There are 65,302 _____

_____.

There are 37,436 fewer _____

_____.

How many _____

_____?

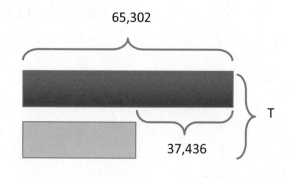

65,302

37,436

T

Lesson 19:   Create and solve multi-step word problems from given tape
Date: diagrams and equations.
                  6/28/13

1.F.31

3. Use the following tape diagram to create a word problem to solve for the missing variable.

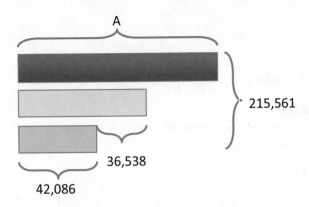

4. Use the equation 27,894 + A + 6,892 = 40,392 to model a tape diagram, create a word problem, and solve.

Lesson 19:   Create and solve multi-step word problems from given tape
                diagrams and equations.
Date: 6/28/13

© 2013 Common Core, Inc. All rights reserved. **commoncore.org**

1.F.32

Name _____   Date _____

1.

    a.   Arrange the following numbers in order, beginning with the smallest.

          504,054   4,450   505,045   44,500

    b.   Use the words "ten times" to tell how you ordered the two smallest numbers using words, pictures and numbers.

2.   Compare using >, <, or =. Place your answer inside the circle.

    a.   1 hundred thousand   ◯   10,000

    b.   200 thousands 4 hundreds   ◯   204,000

    c.   7 hundreds + 4 thousands + 27   ◯   6 thousands + 4 hundreds

    d.   1,000,000   ◯   10 hundred thousands

3. Louisiana State University's Football Stadium has a seating capacity of 92,542.

   a. According to the 2010 census, the population of San Jose, CA was approximately ten times the amount of people that LSU's stadium can seat. What was the population of San Jose?

   b. Write the seating capacity of the LSU stadium in words and in expanded form.

   c. Draw two separate number lines to round the LSU stadium's seating capacity to the nearest ten thousand and to the nearest thousand.

   d. Compare the stadium's seating rounded to the nearest ten thousand and the seating rounded to the nearest thousand using >, <, or =.

   e. Which estimate (rounding to the nearest ten thousand or nearest thousand) is more accurate? Use words and numbers to explain.

Mid-Module Assessment Task Standards Addressed				Topics A–C

Generalize place value understanding for multi-digit whole numbers.

4.NBT.1 Recognize that in a multi-digit whole number, a digit in one place represents ten times what it represents in the place to its right. *For example, recognize that 700 ÷ 70 = 10 by applying concepts of place value and division.*

4.NBT.2 Read and write multi-digit whole numbers using base-ten numerals, number names, and expanded form. Compare two multi-digit numbers based on meanings of the digits in each place, using >, =, and < symbols to record the results of comparisons.

4.NBT.3 Use place value understanding to round multi-digit whole numbers to any place.

Evaluating Student Learning Outcomes

A Progression Toward Mastery chart is provided to describe steps that illuminate the gradually increasing understandings that students develop *on their way to proficiency.* In this chart, this progress is presented from left (Step 1) to right (Step 4). The learning goal for each student is to achieve Step 4 mastery. These steps are meant to help teachers and students identify and celebrate what the student CAN do now, and what they need to work on next.

A Progression Toward Mastery				
Assessment Task Item and Standards Assessed	**STEP 1** **Little evidence of reasoning without a correct answer.** (1 Point)	**STEP 2** **Evidence of some reasoning without a correct answer.** (2 Points)	**STEP 3** **Evidence of some reasoning with a correct answer or evidence of solid reasoning with an incorrect answer.** (3 Points)	**STEP 4** **Evidence of solid reasoning with a correct answer.** (4 Points)
1 **4.NBT.1**	The student is unable to arrange any numbers and does not provide an explanation.	The student arranged two numbers in order, or arranged the least and greatest numbers correctly with providing some explanation of "ten times."	The student arranged three or four numbers correctly but was unable to articulate the relationship of the two smallest numbers using the words "ten times."	The student correctly: ■ Arranged the numbers in the following order: 4,450, 44,500, 504,054, 505,045. ■ Used the words "ten times" to describe the relationship between 4,450 and 44,500.

A Progression Toward Mastery

2 **4.NBT.2**	The student correctly answered one problem.	The student correctly answered two problems.	The student correctly answered three problems.	The student correctly answered all four problems: a. > b. < c. < d. =
3 **4.NBT.1** **4.NBT.2** **4.NBT.3**	The student correctly answered one part, or was able to answer some parts with partial accuracy.	The student correctly answered two of the four parts.	The student correctly answered parts a, b, and c, but was unable to reason in part d.	The student correctly answered all four problems: a. 925,420 b. 90,000 + 2,000 + 500 + 40 + 2. Ninety-two thousand five hundred forty-two. c. Draws two number lines showing the number rounded to 90,000 and 93,000. d. 90,000 < 93,000 e. Explains rounding to the nearest thousand is most accurate because rounding to a smaller unit gives a more accurate estimate so the difference will be closer to the exact number.

Name ___Jack_____   Date _____

1. a. Arrange the following numbers in order, beginning with the smallest.

    504,054   4,450   505,045   44,500

    4,450   44,500   504,054   505,045

    smallest ──────────────────────────→ greatest

   b. Use the words "ten times" to tell how you ordered the two smallest numbers using words, pictures and numbers.

   44,500 is ten times 4,450 so it comes after 4,450 when going from smallest to greatest.

TTh	Th	H	T	O
	4	4	5	0
4	4	5	0	0

   Because 44,500 is ten times 4,450, the digits shift left one place value.

2. Compare using >, <, or =. Place your answer inside the circle.

   a. 1 hundred thousand   (>)   10,000

      100,000

   b. 200 thousands 4 hundreds   (<)   204,000

      200,400

   c. 7 hundreds + 4 thousands + 27   (<)   6 thousands + 4 hundreds

      4,727   6,400

   d. 1,000,000   (=)   10 hundred thousands

3. Louisiana State University's Football Stadium has a seating capacity of 92,542.

   a. According to the 2010 census, the population of San Jose, CA was approximately ten times the amount of people that LSU's stadium can seat. What was the population of San Jose?

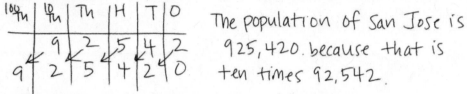

   The population of San Jose is 925,420. because that is ten times 92,542.

   b. Write the seating capacity of the LSU stadium in words and in expanded form.

   90,000 + 2,000 + 500 + 40 +2
   Ninety two thousand five hundred forty two.

   c. Draw two separate number lines to round the LSU stadium's seating capacity to the nearest ten thousand and to the nearest thousand.

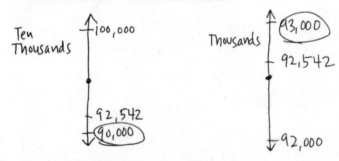

   Ten Thousands
   100,000
   92,542
   90,000

   Thousands
   93,000
   92,542
   92,000

   d. Compare the stadium's seating rounded to the nearest ten thousand and the seating rounded to the nearest thousand using >, <, or =.

   90,000 < 93,000

   e. Which estimate (rounding to the nearest ten thousand or nearest thousand) is more accurate? Use words and numbers to explain.

   Rounding to the nearest thousands is more accurate because the actual number, 92,542, is closer to 93,000 than 90,000. Rounding to a smaller place value is more accurate because it will be closer to the actual number. That's why for this problem, rounding to the thousands gave me an estimate closer to the actual number than rounding to the ten thousands.

Name _____   Date _____

1. Compare the values of each 7 in the number 771,548. Use pictures, numbers and words to explain.

2. Compare using >, <, or =. Place your answer inside the circle.

    a. 234 thousands + 7 ten-thousands   〇   241,000

    b. 4 hundred thousands - 2 thousands   〇   200,000

    c. 1 million   〇   4 hundred thousands + 6 hundred thousands

    d. 709 thousands - 1 hundred thousand   〇   708 thousands

3. Norfolk, VA has a population of 242,628 people. Baltimore, MD has 376,865 more people than Norfolk. Charleston, SC has 496,804 less people than Baltimore.

   a. What is the total population of all three cities? Draw a tape diagram to model the word problem. Then solve the problem.

   b. Round to the nearest hundred thousand to check the reasonableness of your answer for the population of Charleston, SC.

   c. Record each city's population in numbers, in words, and in expanded form.

   d. Compare the population of Norfolk and Charlestown using >, <, or =.

   e. Eddie lives in Fredericksburg, VA, which has a population of 24,286. He says that Norfolk's population is about 10 times as large as Fredericksburg's population. Explain Eddie's thinking.

End–of–Module Assessment Task	Topics A–F
Standards Addressed	

Use the four operations with whole numbers to solve problems.

4.OA.3   Solve multistep word problems posed with whole numbers and having whole-number answers using the four operations, including problems in which remainders must be interpreted. Represent these problems using equations with a letter standing for the unknown quantity. Assess the reasonableness of answers using mental computation and estimation strategies including rounding.

Generalize place value understanding for multi-digit whole numbers.

4.NBT.1   Recognize that in a multi-digit whole number, a digit in one place represents ten times what it represents in the place to its right. *For example, recognize that 700 ÷ 70 = 10 by applying concepts of place value and division.*

4.NBT.2   Read and write multi-digit whole numbers using base-ten numerals, number names, and expanded form. Compare two multi-digit numbers based on meanings of the digits in each place, using >, =, and < symbols to record the results of comparisons.

4.NBT.3   Use place value understanding to round multi-digit whole numbers to any place.

Use place value understanding and properties of operations to perform multi-digit arithmetic.

4.NBT.4   Fluently add and subtract multi-digit whole numbers using the standard algorithm.

Evaluating Student Learning Outcomes

A Progression Toward Mastery is provided to describe steps that illuminate the gradually increasing understandings that students develop *on their way to proficiency.* In this chart, this progress is presented from left (Step 1) to right (Step 4). The learning goal for each student is to achieve Step 4 mastery. These steps are meant to help teachers and students identify and celebrate what the student CAN do now, and what they need to work on next.

A Progression Toward Mastery				
Assessment Task Item and Standards Addressed	**STEP 1** Little evidence of reasoning without a correct answer. (1 Point)	**STEP 2** Evidence of some reasoning without a correct answer. (2 Points)	**STEP 3** Evidence of some reasoning with a correct answer or evidence of solid reasoning with an incorrect answer. (3 Points)	**STEP 4** Evidence of solid reasoning with a correct answer. (4 Points)
1 4.NBT.1	The student is unable to reason about their relationship.	The student can reason about the relationship between two of the 7s, but cannot reason among all three and show a supporting picture or numbers.	The student is able to reason about the relationship of the 7s but their reasoning does not fully support their picture or numbers.	Student correctly reasons the 7 in the hundred thousands place is 10 times the value of the 7 in the ten thousands place. They use a picture or numbers to explain.
2 4.NBT.2 4.NBT.4	The student correctly answers **one** of the **four** parts.	The student correctly answers **two** of the **four** parts.	The student correctly answers **three** of the **four** parts.	The student correctly answers all **four** parts: a. > b. > c. = d. <
3 4.NBT.1 4.NBT.2 4.NBT.3 4.NBT.4 4.OA.3	The student correctly answers **one** of the **four** parts.	The student correctly answers **two** of the **four** parts.	The student answers **three** of the **four** parts correctly.	The student correctly answers all **four** parts: Total population of the three cities combined is 984,810. a. Baltimore's population rounded to the nearest hundred thousand is 600,000. If the population of Charleston is 496,804 less than Baltimore, that can be rounded to 500,000. 600,000 - 500,000 = 100,000. Therefore, 122,689 is a reasonable answer for population of Charleston. 122,689 rounded to the

Module 1:   Place Value, Rounding, and Algorithms for Addition and Subtraction
Date: 6/28/13

A Progression Toward Mastery

				nearest hundred thousand is 100,000.
				b. Charleston, SC- One hundred twenty-two thousand, six hundred eighty-nine. 100,000 + 20,000 + 2,000 + 600 + 80 + 9. Baltimore, MD- Six hundred nineteen thousand four hundred ninety-three. 600,000 + 10,000 + 9,000 + 400 + 90 + 3. Norfolk, VA- Two hundred forty-two thousand six hundred twenty-eight. 200,000 + 40,000 + 2,000 + 600 + 20 + 8.
				c. Norfolk, 242,628 > Charleston, 122,689
				d. Eddie is correct to think that Norfolk's population is 10 times that of Fredericksburg's because Norfolk's population is about 240,000 while Fredericksburg's is about 24,000. 240,000 is ten times larger than 24,000.

Name ___Jack_____   Date _____

1. Compare the values of each 7 in the number 771,548. Use pictures, numbers and words to explain.

The 7 in the hundred thousands place is ten times the value of the 7 in the ten thousands place.

$$70,000 \times 10 = 700,000$$

100Th	10Th	Th	H	T	O
7	7	1	5	4	8
7	0	0	0	0	0
	7	0	0	0	0
		1	0	0	0
			5	0	0
				4	0
					8

2. Compare using >, <, or =. Place your answer inside the circle.

a. 234 thousands + 7 ten-thousands �(>) 241,000

```
  234,000
+  70,000
---------
  304,000
```

b. 4 hundred thousands - 2 thousands (>) 200,000

```
    9
  3 10 10
  4 0 0,000
-     2,000
----------
  398,000
```

c. 1 million (=) 4 hundred thousands + 6 hundred thousands

```
  400,000
+ 600,000
---------
1,000,000
```

d. 709 thousands - 1 hundred thousand   (<) 708 thousands

```
  709,000
- 100,000
---------
  609,000
```

3. Norfolk, VA has a population of 242,628 people. Baltimore, MD has 376,865 more people than Norfolk. Charleston, SC has 496,804 less people than Baltimore.

a. What is the total population of all three cities? Draw a tape diagram to model the word problem. Then solve the problem.

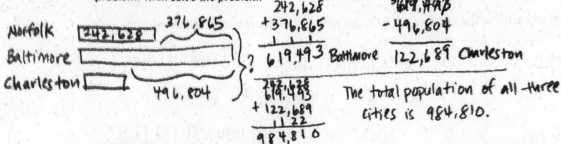

$$242,628$$
$$+376,865$$
$$\overline{619,493} \text{ Baltimore}$$

$$619,493$$
$$-496,804$$
$$\overline{122,689} \text{ Charleston}$$

$$242,628$$
$$619,493$$
$$+122,689$$
$$\overline{984,810}$$

The total population of all three cities is 984,810.

b. Round to the nearest hundred thousand to check the reasonableness of your answer for the population of Charleston, SC.

Baltimore rounded to the nearest hundred thousand is 600,000.
If Charleston is 496,804 less, that can be rounded to 500,000.

600,000 - 500,000 = 100,000   The population of Charleston as

122,689 is a reasonable answer because 122,689 rounded to the nearest hundred thousand is 100,000.

c. Record each city's population in numbers, in words, and in expanded form.

Baltimore: 619,493   Six hundred nineteen thousand, four hundred ninety-three
600,000 + 10,000 + 9,000 + 400 + 90 + 3

Norfolk: 242,628   Two hundred forty-two thousand, six hundred twenty-eight
200,000 + 40,000 + 2,000 + 600 + 20 + 8

Charleston: 122,689   One hundred twenty-two thousand, six hundred eighty-nine
100,000 + 20,000 + 2,000 + 600 + 80 + 9

d. Compare the population of Norfolk and Charlestown using >, <, or =.

Norfolk   Charleston
242,628 > 122,689

e. Eddie lives in Fredericksburg, VA, which has a population of 24,286. He says that Norfolk's population is about 10 times as large as Fredericksburg's population. Explain Eddie's thinking.

Eddie's thinking is correct because Norfolk's population is 242,628 which can be rounded to 240,000. Fredericksburg's population can be rounded to 24,000. 240 thousands is ten times as large as 24 thousands.

100Th	10Th	Th	H	T	O
	2	4	2	8	6
2	4	2	6	2	8